The Dragon Can't Dance

Also in this series

The Dragon Can't Dance

Earl Lovelace

Longman

Longman Group Limited
Longman House,
Burnt Mill, Harlow, Essex, UK

First published by André Deutsch 1979
First published in Longman Drumbeat 1981
Reprinted 1981

ISBN 0 582 64231 0

Printed in Hong Kong by
Commonwealth Printing Press Ltd

For Stephen Charles of Matura
and for Donald, Greg and Spanish

Contents

Prologue

THE HILL

This is the hill tall above the city where Taffy, a man who say he is Christ, put himself úp on a cross one burning midday and say to his followers: 'Crucify me! Let me die for my people. Stone me with stones as you stone Jesus, I will love you still.' And when they start to stone him in truth he get vex and start to cuss: 'Get me down! Get me down!' he say. 'Let every sinnerman bear his own blasted burden; who is I to die for people who ain't have sense enough to know that they can't pelt a man with big stones when so much little pebbles lying on the ground.'

This is the hill, Calvary Hill, where the sun set on starvation and rise on potholed roads, thrones for stray dogs that you could play banjo on their rib bones, holding garbage piled high like a cathedral spire, sparkling with flies buzzing like torpedoes; and if you want to pass from your yard to the road you have to be a high-jumper to jump over the gutter full up with dirty water, and hold your nose. Is noise whole day. Laughter is not laughter; it is a groan coming from the bosom of these houses – no – not houses, shacks that leap out of the red dirt and stone, thin like smoke, fragile like kite paper, balancing on their rickety pillars as broomsticks on the edge of a juggler's nose.

This is the hill, swelling and curling like a machauel snake from Observatory Street to the mango fields in the back of Morvant, its guts stretched to bursting with a thousand narrow streets and alleys and lanes and traces and holes, holding the people who come on the edge of this city to make it home.

This hill is it; and in it; in Alice Street, named for Princess Alice, the Queen's aunt – Alice – soft word on the lips, is a yard before which grows a governor plum tree that has battled its way up through the tough red dirt and stands now, its roots spread out like claws, gripping the earth, its leaves rust red and green, a bouquet in this desert place: a tree bearing fruit that never ripens for Miss Olive's seven, and the area's other children, lean and hard like whips, their wise yellowed eyes filled with malnutrition and too early knowing – innocence was in the womb – children imitating the grown-up laughter and the big-man pose of their elders, who survive here, holding their poverty as a possession, tending it stubbornly as Miss Cleothilda tends her flower garden, clasping it to their bosom as a pass-key whose function they only half-remembered now, and, grown rusty, they wore as jewellery, a charm, a charmed medallion whose magic invested them with a mysterious purity, made them the blue-bloods of a resistance lived by their ancestors all through slavery, carried on in their unceasing escape – as Maroons, as Runways, as Bush Negroes, as Rebels: and when they could not perform in space that escape that would take them away from the scene of their brutalization they took a stand in the very guts of the slave plantation, among tobacco and coffee and cotton and canes, asserting their humanness in the most wonderful acts of sabotage they could imagine and perform, making a religion of laziness and neglect and stupidity and waste: singing hosannahs for flood and hurricane and earthquake, praying for damage and pestilence: continuing it still after Emancipation, that emancipated them to a more profound idleness and waste when, refusing to be grist for the mill of the colonial machinery that kept on grinding in its belly people to spit out sugar and cocoa and copra, they turned up this hill to pitch camp here on the eyebrow of the enemy, to cultivate again with no less fervor the religion with its Trinity of Idleness, Laziness and Waste, so that now, one hundred and twenty-five years after Emancipation, Aldrick Prospect, an aristocrat in this tradition, not knowing where his next meal was coming from, would get up at midday from sleep, yawn, stretch, then start to think of where he might get something to eat, his brain working in the same smooth unhurried nonchalance with which he moved his feet, a slow, cruising crawl which he quickened only at Carnival.

CARNIVAL

Carnival it is that springs this hill alive. Right after Christmas young men get off street corners where they had watched and waited, rubber-tipped sticks peeping out of their back pockets, killing time in dice games, watching the area high-school girls ripening, holding over them the promise of violence and the threat of abuse to keep them respectful, to discourage them from passing them by with that wonderful show of contempt such schoolgirls seem to be required to master to lift them above these slums and these 'hooligans', their brethren, standing at street corners, watching the road grow richer with traffic, the drains float down their filth, holding their backs pressed against the sides of shop buildings from dawn until the scream of police jeeps drive them sullenly on the run, to bring into their waiting a sense of dangerousness and adventure they are happy to embrace, since in these daily police raids they see as much an acknowledgement of their presence as an effort to wrench from them sovereignty of these streets. This moves them to strain all the harder to hold their poses on the walls, to keep alive their visibility and aliveness. And these walls to which they return as soon as the police have driven off, their ritual harassment complete, become more their territory, these walls on which they have scrawled their own names and that of their gangs, Marabuntas, Apple-Jackers, Brimstone, Shane – hard names derived from the movies which on some nights they slip off the walls to see, Western movies of the gun talk and the quick draw and the slow crawl, smooth grand gestures which they imitate so exquisitely as though those gestures were their own borrowed to the movie stars for them to later reclaim as proper to their person, that person that leans against the wall, one foot drawn up to touch the thigh, the hat brim turned down, the eyelid half closed, the body held in that relaxed aliveness, like a deer, watching the world from under the street lamp whose bulb they dutifully shatter as soon as it is changed: that person savouring his rebellion as a ripe starch mango, a matchstick fixed between his teeth at an angle that he alone could measure, and no one imitate.

With Carnival now, they troop off street corners, desert their battlefield and territory, and turn up the hill to the steelband tent to assemble before steel drums cut to various lengths and tuned and fashioned to give out the dif- ferent tones – bass, alto, cello – instruments that had their beginnings in kerosene tins, biscuit drums, anything that could sound a note, anything that could ring; metal drums looted from roadsides, emptied of their garbage and pressed into service to celebrate the great war's end, and to accompany the calypsonian's instant song: It's your mous- tache we want, Hitler.

Now, the steelband tent will become a cathedral, and these young men priests. They will draw from back pockets those rubber-tipped sticks, which they had carried around all year, as the one link to the music that is their life, their soul, and touch them to the cracked faces of the drums. Hours, hours; days, days; for weeks they beat these drums, beat these drums, hammering out from them a cry, the cry, the sound, stroking them more gently than they will ever caress a woman; and then they have it. At last, they have it. They have the tune that will sing their person and their pose, that will soar over the hill, ring over the valley of shacks, and laugh the hard tears of their living when, for Carnival, they enter Port of Spain.

CALYPSO

Up on the hill with Carnival coming, radios go on full blast, trembling these shacks, booming out calypsos, the songs that announce in this season the new rhythms for people to walk in, rhythms that climb over the red dirt and stone, break-away rhythms that laugh through the groans of these sights, these smells, that swim through the bones of these enduring people so that they shout: Life! They cry: Hurrah! They drink a rum and say: Fuck it! They walk with a tall hot beauty between the garbage and dog shit, proclaiming life, exulting in the bare bones of their person and their skin.

Up on the hill with Carnival coming and calypso tunes swimming in the hair of these shacks, piercing their nostrils, everybody catches the spirit and these women with baskets and with their heads tied, these women winding daily down this hill on which no buses run, tramping down this asphalt lane slashed across this mountain's face, on their way, to Port of Spain city, to market, to work as a domestic, or to any other menial task they inherit because of their beauty; these women, in this season, bounce with that tall delicious softness of bosom and hip, their movements a dance, as if they were earth priestesses heralding a new spring.

The children dance too, coming home from school in the hot afternoon when the sun has cooked the castles of dog shit well, so that its fumes rise like incense proper to these streets. They dance, skipping along, singing calypsos whose words they know by heart already, swishing their skirt tails, moving their waists, laughing, their laughter scattering like shells into the hard flesh of the hill. Dance! There is dancing in the calypso. Dance! If the words mourn the death of a neighbour, the music insists that you dance; if it tells the troubles of a brother, the music says dance. Dance to the hurt! Dance! If you catching hell, dance, and the government don't care, dance! Your woman take your money and run away with another man, dance. Dance! Dance! Dance! It is in dancing that you ward off evil. Dancing is a chant that cuts off the power from the devil. Dance! Dance! Dance! Carnival brings this dancing to every crevice on this hill.

The Dragon Can't Dance

I Queen of the Band

For the whole year here in the yard on Alice Street, Miss Cleothilda, the mulatto woman occupying the two front rooms upstairs the main house, has lived, tending her flowers and fern hanging in wire baskets from the ceiling of the narrow verandah, scolding her brown and white pup over its toilet training, fussing, and criticizing everything – the ugliness of the area, the noise of the children climbing the governor plum tree – making a nuisance of herself to everybody, strutting about the yard with her rouged cheeks and padded hips, husbanding her fading beauty, flaunting her gold bangles and twin gold rings that proclaim that she was once married, wearing dresses, showing her knees, that if you give her a chance will show her thighs, walking this street on her way from market with her overflowing basket, displaying her more expensive purchases – the crab and the callaloo bush and the bound legs of the white chicken and the fat fingers of yellow plantains – her nose lifted above the city, her long hair plaited in two plaits, like a schoolgirl, choking with that importance and beauty which she maintained as a queenship which not only she, but the people who shared the yard with her, had the duty to recognize and responsibility to uphold. She owned a little parlour stocked with goods ranging from haberdashery to groceries, and she ran it as if she were doing a favour to the Hill rather than carrying on a business from which she intended to profit: closing and opening whenever she pleased, holding up the steady stream of customers to lecture anyone who dared come in without first saying good morning, leaving her enduring customers unattended to go and feed her dog or chat with one of her old friends who periodically dropped in, reserving the full cutting mischief of her tongue for anyone who dared suggest that she should hurry.

All year long she carried on hostile, superior and un-accommodating, refusing still from the height of her presumed gentility to give even recognition far less en-couragement to Philo, the calypsonian across the street, who, by whatever miracle of endurance and shamelessness and hope, after seventeen years still nursed this passion for her, dismissing him with that brisk turn of her head, the raising of her eyelashes and the sucking of her teeth, in one fluid gesture of disgust that she could perform better than anybody else. But, now that it was Carnival season, Miss Cleothilda was getting friendly with everybody. In the same swirling spasm of energy that fueled her earlier pose, she had become a saint almost, giving away sweets to the children, questioning them about their lessons, advis-ing them against the perils of the Hill in a voice loud enough so that adults near by could hear, holding the little boys and girls speechless and tame, their round eyes printed on her face, which she knew how to so wonderfully change to dramatize whatever point she chose to make.

She had already made her journey to the steelband tent, a few streets farther up the Hill, to view the sketches of the masquerade costume the band would appear in for Car-nival, and had given her decision: she would portray the queen − queen of the band − though the Hill was by now certain that she would never appear in any other costume; for the Hill knew that it was not only a habit − she had been playing queen for the last eleven years − nor that she could afford it; the Hill knew what she knew: that to her being queen was not really a masquerade at all, but the annual affirming of a genuine queenship that she accepted as hers by virtue of her poise and beauty, something acknowledged even by her enemies, something that was not identical with her mulattohood, but certainly impossible without it. And now assuming the mantle of her queenship, she would be all laughter and excitement. Now she would come out on her verandah and stand below her potted flowers, her thin legs in shorts, her wrinkled knees showing her years more truthfully than her face, and in a honeyed voice thrilling with excitement she would call out to Miss Olive, the stout slow watchful woman who lived downstairs from her in two rooms and the everlasting bedlam of her seven children, call out to her to listen to the latest calypso coming over the radio whose volume she (Cleothilda) had turned up to a booming pitch the better to advertise her generosity; and, as if to add conviction to this gesture of concern, of friendliness, to show how fully she had become one with the yard in this season, she would throw her hands in the air, step off a pace or two and do a dance, shaking her waist and twisting her body to the music in that delightful flourish of middle-aged sexiness that she knew would draw a pleasing laughter from people in the yard below.

'You hear rhythm, Miss Olive? You hear song? Carnival!' she would cry out. 'Bachanal! Trinidad! All o' we is one.'

And, with the eyes of the yard upon her, and just a bit breathless from her efforts, she would pause, assuming now a tone of seriousness, already intent on contradicting an unvoiced objection, and shout for the whole yard to hear: 'Miss Olive, we is all one people. No matter what they say, all o' we is one,' sanctifying this sentiment, expressed now in song year after year by the island's leading calypsonians, with her own blessings, strengthening it in its march to being the anthem it would become. And Miss Olive who would have come out into the yard at her call, dutiful as always, and would have witnessed the performance, would stand looking up at her, in that tall loose unease; and she would smile in a bashful sort of suspicious way, her wide nose flared above her lips, asserting in that response that she would never be able to fathom Miss

Cleothilda, saying to herself: I wonder if Miss Cleothilda really crazy, or if this rush of friendliness is the first instalment on her masquerade for Carnival day.

For years Miss Olive had wanted to ask Miss Cleothilda this question to her face, but each time she looked into Miss Cleothilda's eyes, the question on her lips, she had felt a sense of Miss Cleothilda's fragility. It seemed to her although she was the one discomfited by Miss Cleothilda's usage, that despite the harshness Miss Cleothilda projected throughout the ordinary year; indeed, because of it – there was in her a lack of human toughness to face real life as a real person. She seemed to feel the need to steal up on it, outwit it. She had to race around and try to confuse it. Miss Olive would feel so embarrassed by this knowledge that she sensed it would be unkind to confront Miss Cleothilda with a question whose answer must unclothe, unveil Cleothilda, perhaps even to her own self. More than that, she believed that she had waited too long to demand an explanation, and that demanding one so late now would be a betrayal of a kind of trust Miss Cleothilda had in her, a belief in her dependability, in the fact that she would accept her no matter what she said or did to her. Miss Olive found herself forced into the position of that person who now seeks to prevent from going through her yard a trespasser whom she had watched make it a thoroughfare, acquiring in such usage a right of passage that not even a law suit could take away. Yet, Miss Olive did not like the seasonal nature of Miss Cleothilda's affection and concern. She was bothered by this trespassing against her person, this dependability on her passivity. The trespasser had not only used her yard as a thoroughfare, she had widened it into a highway.

'I going to ask her the question,' she said to Miss Caroline, her neighbour in the next yard, over the fence, in reply to Caroline's withering outraged gaze as Miss Cleothilda turned inside after her performance. 'I getting too old to be jumping when she call. I getting too tired to fix on my face a smile that I don't feel, and pretend that she and me is friends when she come out on her verandah and shake her waist.'

'But you don't have to ask the woman anything, Olive,' Caroline said, unbottling her vexation in a stream of talk that would flow unceasing even when she paused to take a breath, its echoes continuing on, surrounding, like the flapping of bats flying around in an empty room. 'You don't have eyes in your head to see that is because the woman skin lighter than yours and mine she feel she better than people on this Hill. And all the friendly-friendly thing she give off for Carnival is just a smoke-screen to hide the wretch she really is, to make you forget long enough the things she do all through the year, to relax you, so she could come again and lord she-self over you, and push her finger in your eye again. And we, so stupid and without shame, ready to embrace her again, every Carnival, without asking no question or she giving no explanation; so she ain't have no stop, no halt, no slowing down. She ain't have nothing to make her wonder if what she doing is right, if she living life as a human being. I tell you, Olive, Cleothilda will never like me. First I don't credit at her place. She can't twist me and turn me as she do you and Philo. And Philo! Philo such a jackass at his age, up in the woman tail, and she don't want him. She don't want him, you know. And what make her precious so? That fading yellow red-nigger skin? 'Cause she ain't no spring chicken again. Is seventeen years since she place third in the Carnival Queen competition in Port of Spain: two white girls, one first, the other second, and the girl, a black girl who come in as Miss Ebony and who shoulda win the whole thing, fourth, and she third – seventeen years ago and Philo, since that time have in him this thing for her, this love or lust or what the hell it is. And Philo is not a bad-looking man. Black as he is, when he put on clothes and comb his hair he could get any reasonable woman; but is she he want. Seventeen years he coming in this yard every day and calling out to her and she insulting him to his face: she don't want no calypso man! Why he don't go and look for a woman of his class? And, tell me, what class she is? What class? Philo is a jackass in a jackass skin, smiling at the insults she shower on him, but only let me raise my voice a little and talk too hard to him, he ready to cuff me through the partition. Oh, he will smile at all the insults from that woman, waiting for Carnival to come so he could jump in the band and put his hand round her waist and shout, 'All o' we is one'; and the fool don't know that that is all he going to ever get. That it is the same way she treat everybody who blacker than she: lording it over them for the whole year, and for Carnival, coming out and pretending that she and you is friend.

'She will never like me because she know I up to her tricks. And even that fool Philo, I could understand, running like a dog up her steps when Carnival come and she invite him in for a drink. He blind. In all these years the farthest she allow him is on her verandah. Three steps a year is the quota she give him, and he climbing them steps as if they is the fourteen stations of the cross; so that last year he reach her verandah, so at that rate it will take him maybe fifteen – what I saying? – twenty more years to get in the room that she have her bed in, which is where he think he heading. Twenty more years before he reach to glory. But with she drying up like a old prune already, and he 'self ain't getting no younger, I don't know what kinda glory that will be. I sympathize with him. That woman is like a sickness hook on inside him; but, you, Olive? What it is that have you bowing to her so? What preventing you from putting she in her place? Or maybe you really feel she is some kinda queen. You really feel she ain't have no responsibility to live and be a human being. I tell you: you don't have to credit from her. The Chinese man will let you open an account with him.'

'Yes,' Miss Olive said. 'Yes. I ain't taking no more foolishness from that woman.'

And, really, in her heart, she meant it. At Miss Cleothilda's next call she stepped into the yard with a slow,
righteous combativeness; but, the moment she lifted her
head and saw Cleothilda on her verandah, with her costume
on and with that sense of gleeful delight, her resolve fell
away. A kind of pity moved her. She didn't have the heart to
hurt Miss Cleothilda. So, it was, she reached again for the
consoling thought: Miss Cleothilda not right in her head.
She felt in herself a strength, a wisdom. She felt that
between the two of them, she and Cleothilda, she was the
stronger and the tougher and the older and the one that
would prevail. Caroline, she felt, didn't understand.

So Miss Olive was content to smile and enjoy Miss
Cleothilda's performance on her verandah, suffering herself to bear Caroline's looks of accusation from across the
fence. Caroline was too hurry. Life wasn't going nowhere.
Let Miss Cleothilda carry on until her rope reached its end.
But to Miss Olive's daughter, Sylvia, at seventeen, ripening like a mango rose, watching from one corner of the
yard, snapping her fingers, tapping her feet to the calypso
music prancing in her brain, Miss Cleothilda's performance done on her verandah in her shimmering bodice of
black and gold brought the full excitement and panic of the
approaching Carnival.

2   The Princess

Sylvia ain't have no man. At seventeen, in the height of preparations for Carnival, the Hill hot, loud, buzzing with beating steelband people walking in calypso rhythm, proclaiming their aliveness, and, in the yard, Miss Cleothilda gushing with a jubilant friendliness, showing off on her verandah the sketches of her masquerade costume and later on the costume itself, putting on a one woman fashion show on her gallery below her ferns and flowers in wire pots, showing now her satin cape, now her sword, now her slippers dusted in gold, dancing, shaking her body to the music coming over her radio, squealing with delight, rubbing in her excitement as she went through those movements she would make on Carnival day when as Queen she would be out on the street at the head of the band underneath the banners and the flying flags; Sylvia is dizzy with thoughts of Carnival. They are bursting in her brain. Everywhere she turns the young men of the area, who have grown up with her, turn and ask her: 'Sylvia, you playing in the band?' their eyes sweeping up her ankles, along the softening curves of her thighs and breasts, desiring her, wishing, each one of them, to have her jumping up with him in the band for Carnival, when, with the help of rum and the rhythm of abandon and surrender that conquered everyone he would find his way into her flesh.

A few of them had already delved fumbling hands beneath her dress, a few of them, growing up here in this tight space, this hot hard yard; but even so she was always too quick for them, too much the humming-bird blur; and her mind was never in it, and she had watched the whole act, felt the trembling knees, the groping hands, the hard thing scraping against the web of fine hair butting around, trying with no help from her to pierce the dark crevice between her thighs. She had watched, felt, the whole performance as if she wasn't there, from a distance, was already engaged in the apprenticeship of being the whore, the virgin fucked but untouched.

Already she had outgrown these boys that never sliced her virginity. She had grown away from them, and, even before them, the men watching her, so that now she could look at all of them with a kind of amusement, wonder, really, watching to see what they would try next. Once Mr Guy had felt her breasts, cupping them in his hands in that sly cunning hug, pretending fatherly affection; and one day she had crept upstairs to his room while he waited for her behind his curtains, his moustaches trembling and his radio on, and she had given him the message: her mother didn't have the money for the rent. Afterwards, she had lifted her downcast eyes to his as she felt his thick fingers slide up and down her thigh in that gesture of aggression and taming, as his chest rose and his nostrils flared; and she smiled, laughed in that same knowing innocence, that feigned play in which he couched his advances to her, and slipped away. Next day he came downstairs to tell her mother: 'Your rent is okay, Miss Olive.' And there was in her even then no shame as she looked up at him, shaved and neat, his hair well parted and his tie hanging down his chest, for she knew then, already, with that instinctive knowing refined by seventeen years on this hill, that between this man, the rent collector, and her mother, a woman with seven children and no man either, she was the gift arranged even before she knew it, even without the encouragement or connivance of her mother. She was the sacrifice. So she would let him pat her on the head, feel his hand sliding down her back going over the hill of her buttocks, and, mischievously, she sometimes stood still, as if she needed to perfect that unflinching steadiness and triumphant surrender fitted for the whoredom that was her destiny, if not her calling.

But she moved too fast for things to penetrate her: they could only slide off her; and she would walk, her young breasts dancing on springs, with that briskness of limb, the whore, the virgin, challenging the fate already laid out for her, getting close to the danger coiled in the crotches of this slum without slowing down or relaxing long enough to let it pierce her; so that the women, the older women who had eyes, who had felt the burnings of this living, would watch her sweeping along with the sunshine dancing on her head, moving with that careless inviting speed and slowness, that bold swinging openness that narrowed men's eyes, would want to take her in their arms to protect her, would want to wish a magic guard over her so that she would not be trampled by this hill; and, as one voice, they would cry out: 'Too fast, Sylvia! Slow down, girl. Slow down. Slow down.' But secretly, in their hearts, they cheered her on, singing hurrahs at her speed and dangerousness and laughing, watching with joyful breathlessness how she tied up the tongues of young men with a movement of her head and caused old men to sigh for their youth as they watched her sitting cross-legged on the steps before the rooms in which she lived, praying, even as they envied and applauded, that she would make the miracle, climb undefeated out of this hill. But with all these young men coming into the yard and asking for Sylvia, with so many eyes pressing down on her, they felt that she was doomed: the miracle they dared to wish was too staggering for their faith; so any day they expected to hear the worst: that she was having a baby, this affliction that swelled you up and dropped your breasts and slashed away your youth and promise; so they would ease up to her, women like Thelma Bridges and Miss Hilda and Miss Caroline, women who knew, and, dropping little hints, they would let her know what she should do if she didn't want that burden, or at whose house to go if she should find herself in the family way. But Sylvia ain't have no man: and these young men hot to get under her dress ain't working nowhere, so when two weeks before Carnival, Mr Guy, ever on the look out for an invitation from her, always watching hawk-eyed for the slightest shift in her mood or attitude that might give him the opening he had begun seeking more auda-ciously now that her breasts had risen into their own two islands – when Mr Guy came upon her standing vacantly at the stand-pipe, her bucket overflowing and her eyes gazing off in space, and said to her: 'Sylvia, you not playing in the band?' she had turned and turned off the tap, bent to lean the bucket to clear it of its overflow the better to carry it, hitched up the elastic at the waist of her panties, the lone garment between her dress and skin, and turned from the bucket of water to look at him, letting her eyes sweep slowly up the insides of his legs, up to his waist in a calm, almost inquiring appraisal that moved Mr Guy to pull his stomach in and stand a little more erect, before she turned again and lifted the bucket by its handles, and, balancing herself with that lean that bent her body sideways towards the bucket, one hand holding the hem of her skirt, she carried the bucket from the pine to the middle of the yard where she stood it to rest near enough to Guy so that a sigh from her could fill his nostrils with her dangerous woman youthfulness.

'What costume you want?' he asked her now, talking in that deep whisper that barely moved his moustaches, his voice promising and pleading, hushing her, edging her into a moist darkness filled with burnings and the smell of sea water. 'And . . . any costume you want, just tell me,' he said, his voice abandoning whatever remained of his elderly authority, investing itself with the full urgency and generosity and wanting of his giving. 'Tonight! Come upstairs tonight, I will give it to you.'

She had lifted her head then, not sharply, drawing back

in the same instant one foot a little so that the hem of her dress stretched between her legs, and looked at him, pausing first, and then saying: ' You making joke, Mr Guy,' the upsweep of her eyes in time with her words, making his nostrils quiver, sniff, flare, and his brain leap to seize upon the thrust and promise of that remark, so that his words when he said them would be almost a plea: 'I ain't joking. You – you want to play a princess? A lady in waiting? Anything!' his voice breaking out of its controlled whisper, rising, betraying his wanting, anxious and full with its promise and plea.

She stood there, one leg drawn back a little behind the other, keeping still the tension in the cloth of her dress, her lower lip tucked into her mouth, her eyes gazing off upstairs at his room, as if measuring the distance and the steepness of the ascent up his steps: gazing there while he let his eyes swim over the firm waves of her flesh down to the taut V her parted legs made in the shadow of the junction of her thighs and body, listening to his whispered offer and wanting cartwheeling about her head, holding her immodest pose, savouring with an innocent delight the fact of her woman-ness, not knowing yet that Miss Cleothilda had appeared on her verandah and was surveying the scene until she heard Guy breathe the hurried question and demand. 'Tonight?' and turn – another person – the mature and pleasant rent collector – towards the house to say in a voice, light and half joking, empty of its earlier dark whispering: 'Miss Cleothilda, what have you looking so nice this morning?' drawing from that woman a maidenly and self-congratulatory acceptance (as he might have nicely anticipated): 'Me? I have to try, Mr Guy. I have to try. I ain't a young girl again. Eh, Sylvia?' Sylvia turning then, turning to confront her with the full innocent and aggravating audacity of her youth and a mischievous surprise: 'What you say, Miss Cleothilda?'

'Nothing girl. Just this old man teasing me,' Miss

Cleothilda, smiling, suggesting that she had spoken simply to let Sylvia know that she shared what was still a secret.

Sylvia seemed unconcerned; and as she bent in that jubilant curtsy to take up her bucket, and Guy started to ease away, Miss Cleothilda intent on blunting Sylvia's triumph and asserting her own power, calls out sweetly, 'Sylvia, wait! I think I have a dress here that could fit you – if your mother would let you take it.' And, without waiting for Sylvia's reply, was already calling in that ringing voice of hers that made every statement of hers a public announcement: 'Miss Olive, Miss Olive! You mind if I give Sylvia a dress?' drawing, with that innocent cunning, Miss Olive out of her house to witness the dissolving scene of her daughter and Mr Guy.

'Sylvia, you want the dress?' Miss Olive asked tiredly. 'Dress? Which dress? I ain't see no dress,' replies Sylvia, striking back with effortlessness a blow that Miss Cleothilda half-hoped would be the first in a battle to uphold her pride against the indignity of accepting the cast-off clothing.

Miss Cleothilda smiled; she really didn't care if Sylvia accepted. She was satisfied simply to establish that she (Cleothilda) was in a position to give, and Sylvia, even if she refused, to receive. 'Oh ho,' she said. 'Why you don't come upstairs and try it on.'

'Okay,' Sylvia answers, off-handedly, as if she was the one doing the favour, so that Miss Cleothilda, feeling robbed of her victory, would say with that joyful slander, 'I know you don't care for dress from me. A girl like you could get anything you want.'

That night, with the steelband humming over the hill, Sylvia left her mother sleeping and crept outside in the hot darkness, barefooted, and with nothing on under her dress, and stood beside the lavatory, alert, poised to move, like a dancer, her eyes searching the yard to see who was about at that hour. Aldrick, going to shut the one window of his little shack, saw her – not her, the figure that could only have been she, since of all the girls in the neighbourhood, only she at standstill and in silhouette could hold and radiate that warm immodest breathlessness – saw her and froze, the better to watch what would take place, not even surprised; for immediately he saw her in that posture at that hour, he had decided with a matter-of-factness, almost relief, already relinquishing the responsibility that he had never acknowledged, that her turn had come; and he stood at the window curious simply to discover which of the young fellows of the area was the lucky one.

In the seventeen years he had lived on this hill he had seen generations of girls graduate from these beginnings to night clubs, to brothels, to the city's streets, to live in that strict and lascivious immodesty, like wrongsided nuns, on their way to becoming battle-axes, the mother superiors of whoredom, irreverent and wise; if they were lucky, dropping their unwanted progeny at the home of a grandmother or aunt or friend, and if they were not, being forced to retire periodically from the scene of their labours to nurse their children. He had seen generations of them go that route, and it always touched him to see another one – the youth, the faith. Now it was Sylvia's turn. The real reason why Aldrick remained at his window as long as he did, quiet as his own shadow, was because that shadow poised and breathless there, that Sylvia, more than any of the hundreds that passed from this hill on the way to their inevitable whoredom, carried with her not only that crazy immodest invincibility, but possessed a fragility, like that contained in finely tuned athletes or racehorses or violins, that was itself an acknowledgement of class, a quality that had chosen her out with that sense of poetry by which oases rise up in deserts and the most delicate flowers select dunghills for their blooming, that signalled directly to him, called out of him a deep primal manness that made him want if he were not careful – to spring to her protection, to say deep soft words to her, to take her into his humble room and begin a dream. He had never had much to do with teenaged girls: they were too much trouble; but Sylvia, he avoided completely. To him she was the most dangerous female person on the Hill, for she possessed, he suspected, the ability not only to capture him in passion but to enslave him in caring, to bring into his world those ideas of love and home and children that he had spent his whole life avoiding. So he had watched her swing back and forth in the yard, not even wanting to meet her eyes, keeping his distance, not even trying to get her into his bed, for he knew that she could make him face questions that he had innoculated himself against by not working nowhere, by not being too deeply concerned about anything except his dragon costume that he prepared for his masquerade on Carnival day.

He was standing there at his window, watching the shadow poised still in its alertness, waiting to see the fellow with whom she would rendezvous, saying in his mind a kind of goodbye, a kind of farewell, a kind of adieu, when he heard Guy cough, a dry, falsetto sound that Aldrick immediately decided was a signal; for the instant it came, the figure in the shadows stirred, turned and looked around, clearing her own throat lightly, the very sound breathing out a warm, moist promise, making him regret that he wasn't the one.

'So Guy is the man,' he thought. 'Guy! The son-fa-bitch, stepping around like a proper gentleman and screwing all the little girls on the Hill! Guy!'

But no. He couldn't let that concern him. That was how things were, and, in a way it was better it was Guy, who could give her a little money and buy her some clothes, than one of those rank little boys who ain't working nowhere and whose panting, honest as it might be, brought to her neither escape nor promise nor security. Better Guy, the son-fa-bitch, who might, if his heart soften, even try to get her a job in a store downtown, give her some kinda protection, some kinda chance to escape this hill. Better Guy, he thought, convincing himself; and he reached for the cigarette he had fitted behind his ear to smoke before he went to bed. But then she must have become aware of his presence. He must have made a noise or something, for he felt this change in her posture, and saw that she was looking in his direction. Instead of turning away and pretending that he had not seen her, he lit his cigarette boldly. As he took the first two puffs, she crossed and came to stand next to his window, her hands grasping the hem of her single garment around her knees.

'So . . .' he said.

'So?' she answered, already combative, drawing back her body, setting her hands on her hips, her head thrown back.

'So Guy is your man?' And as she looked at him, her silence an inquiry, her posture suggesting that her own assault was forthcoming, he added quickly, 'I don't mind, you know. Do what you want, I don't care . . . I ain't going to say nothing.'

'What *you* could say?'

'I could say: a nice girl like you . . .'

'A nice girl like me?'

'Yes,' Aldrick said, 'a nice girl like you – you could get married.'

'You will marry me?' she asked in that same aggressive, combative voice.

'Me? Married! I can't afford a woman. You don't see how I living? No chair, a little bed in a little room. A woman want things. I ain't have nothing here except my dragon costume to put on for Carnival.'

She softened a little then, the wild animal that might have been the prey scenting wavering in the one who might have been predator. 'But you always have woman coming here to you.'

'Yes. But you never see any of them stay more than a night. I can't afford it. I . . . I ain't have nowhere to put them.'

'You can't get a bigger place and buy some chairs? Even in there, you and somebody could live, if you love her.'

Aldrick chuckled softly. 'She will have to eat. I ain't working nowhere.'

And then a silence had fallen between them: he, blowing out his cigarette smoke into it; she, hand on hip, head thrown back, watching him, listening.

'You never was in love, Aldrick?' she asked; and his mind raced in quick review of all the women he had known, women who flitted in and out his life without really touching it, their relations ending in bed, as if they had together come with no more ambition or hope or want beyond a mutual desiring in the flesh, and when that last was satisfied the attraction would disappear. At best they would move away from each other, with nothing added to nothing, with no pain dulled, no burden lightened except the one in his groin.

'No,' he said. 'Love is on the screen.'

'Me neither,' she said. 'I like to see love pictures, though. You feel those people real on the screen, or it is something they make up. I find it does look so real.'

'You like Guy?' he asked.

'He buying a costume for me.'

The silence came again; and up the Hill the steelband had stopped playing.

'It ain't no big costume either, is just that I have to be there in the band when Carnival come. I have to play . . . You finish your dragon costume yet?'

'Nearly,' he said.

'You lucky,' she said. 'You always have your costume. You don't get tired playing the same mas' every year?'

'Every year I make a new costume. The costume this year ain't the one I had last year. When I finish I always throw them away.'

'I know. But, still, in a way is the same costume, the same dragon. I wonder if I could do that?'

'Do what?'

'Play the same masquerade every year.'

'What costume you want?'

'It ain't no big expensive costume. You will laugh when I tell you. A . . . a slave girl,' she said bashfully. 'You see, it ain't no big expensive costume. You feel I should play a princess or a slave girl?'

He smiled. 'You is a princess already,' he said. 'Play a slave girl.'

'I could ask you a question? Don't get vexed, you know.'

'What could get me vex?' he said.

'How? How you make out? I mean, how you manage not working nowhere and you always have women coming to your place?'

He paused. 'I don't know.'

'Well,' she said, 'you not so bad looking.'

'You ain't so bad looking yourself,' he said.

'You feel? You really feel I is a princess in truth?'

'You is a princess.' He meant it, and it sounded in his voice, and she heard it and was silent. He was silent too.

Guy coughed again. Aldrick looked down at the girl. He wished he could see her eyes. Then, from the front room where she lived the light went on.

'Shhh! My mother!' she cried.

At her words she pressed against the window, flattening herself against the wall so that her head was just below Aldrick's chin, and her scent filled his nostrils, and a few strands of her hair brushed against his cheeks. He didn't move. The light went out. Guy coughed again, very softly, and his lights went on and off quickly.

She straightened herself. He was choking. She was all inside him now.

'I better go,' she said.

'Okay,' he managed. He hesitated as if there was something that he should add, wanted to add. 'Okay,' he said again.

She waved, and he turned away from the window and her. He didn't want to see where she was going.

3   The Dragon

With the door of his little shack half open, Aldrick worked solemnly on his dragon costume, saying nothing to Basil, the little boy of ten who came from somewhere in the neighbourhood of Alice Street, appeared just so a year before, in the ragged khaki pants and sleeveless merino that was his uniform all that year, and stood at the door and gazed in at the dragon costume Aldrick was then making, looking from the costume to Aldrick with a fullness of wonderment and fascination and awe, leaving, only when dark fell, to return next day and the next all through the making of the dragon costume, maintaining that attitude of reverence throughout, as if he were in the presence of holiness, until one day Aldrick asked him to run to Miss Cleothilda's parlour and buy him a pack of cigarettes; and cemented in that act the boy's apprenticeship to dragon making. So the boy was here again this year. And, working now, he seemed to divine exactly which tool or piece of material Aldrick needed for his work, and he handed it to him with a ceremonial solemnity as if he, the boy, were an acolyte, and Aldrick the priest.

In truth, it was in a spirit of priesthood that Aldrick addressed his work; for, the making of his dragon costume was to him always a new miracle, a new test not only of his skill but of his faith: for though he knew exactly what he had to do, it was only by faith that he could bring alive from these scraps of cloth and tin that dragon, its mouth breathing fire, its tail threshing the ground, its nine chains rattling, that would contain the beauty and threat and terror that was the message he took each year to Port of Spain. It was in this message that he asserted before the world his self. It was through it that he demanded that others *see* him, recognize his personhood, be warned of his danger-ousness.

Aldrick worked slowly, deliberately; and every thread he sewed, every scale he put on the body of the dragon, was a thought, a gesture, an adventure, a name that celebrated some part of his journey to and his surviving upon this hill. He worked, as it were, in a flood of memories, not trying to assemble them, to link them to get a linear meaning, but letting them soak him through and through; and his life grew before him, in the texture of his paint and the angles of his dragon's scales, as he worked. And, working now, he sewed scales for his grandfather, who he remembered from the far distance of his boyhood on that browning green hill between the giant immortelle trees above the cocoa and dying bananas, a short man, stiff as the varnished straight-backed chair on which he sat in the front room, alone, tall before the table set with his breakfast of eggs and goat's milk and his grandmother's home-made bread and avocado, alone as if the rest of the family, his own wife and daughters and grandchildren, were not fit companions when he broke bread; alone in the front room, the altar of the house, the clean polished room with framed and passe-partouted photographs of members of the family on the walls, and a big one of his brother George who was in America, and one of God Bless This House, with its green cherries and red leaves, hanging near the hat rack with the mirror in it, above the varnished chairs, around the little centre table of cedar upon the polished floor upon which only visitors trod – and not many of them either, certainly, none from the village itself – except for Christ-mas Day when the whole family came into that room smell-ing now of Christmas, smelling now of new curtains and fresh varnish and balloons.

He knitted into his dragon this old man, stern and stiff

and unbending, the last pillar of a falling building, whose slightest shift would collapse the entire structure, puzzling over him, this man, his mother's father, remembering him still holding on then to the five acres of mountain and stone that had exhausted its substance, if it ever had any, years before he bought it, holding on with a passion so fierce that it blinded him to the dwindling size of the fruit the tired brown trees tugged out of the earth, as if the land, that mountain and stone land, held some promise that he alone knew of, that was never revealed to his wife or to his children, and that would be already lost to Aldrick by the time he was old enough to understand; remained with the old man, kept as the photograph of a long departed lover from an affair itself lived, lost, gone – no, rather as the letter from that lover who never came, who had written fifty years before promising that she was coming, and who after fifty years he still kept waiting for, no longer really expecting her to turn up, but continuing to wait in that kind of active martyred hopelessness that seems a hope, reproaching her with his very patience and waiting for every minute of the fifty years, so that if she ever came he could say: I kept my part of the bargain; and if she never came his waiting would be a monument to his faith. For that reason, in the cause of his martyrdom and faith that was not really faith at all but a wicked reproach to the promise of the land, to the promise for which he could only have held God responsible, the waiting man refusing to listen to anyone who suggests that the lover is not coming, he refused to hear anything against the promise of the land. And towards the end, for all the toil and time he had put in on the land with his wife and children and grandchildren, he expected as return not produce, not cocoa or coffee or bananas or oranges, but that he could say to God, who must have been the one to make him the promise: I kept my part of the bargain. You told me to cutlass and hoe and weed and sow; well, I have done all of it. I have kept my part of the bargain.

Immersed in this perverse mission, he ceased to be any kind of flesh and blood man, had become the symbol of an unyielding and triumphant martyrdom, intent on inflicting on his family the land and its promise which he had waited on for fifty years, in vain, so that even when his daughters, the two youngest, were twenty-five and twenty-two, and the avocados were the smallest they had ever been, growing smaller from year to year, and the cocoa field, riddled with witches broom and black pod, was so diseased that no amount of pruning or cutlassing or mulching could rehabilitate: even after all those years of seeing what must have been withering and dying all around him, and the disappearing meaning in the promise that he might have honestly believed in once, even then he would resist their going as the pillar resists the falling of the building it is holding up from toppling.

'The children big now, Cyrus,' his grandmother had said, speaking to him in that moaning tone that had known years of silence, years of being hurled back by the old man's stubborn unyielding faith. 'And the land old and things ain't bearing right, and is all right for we who old, who accustomed to this nothing, who ain't looking for no future from this world . . . I want them to go where they could get a chance to be somebody. Their chance, Cyrus. Their own chance.'

'What?' he asked, irritated as a man just waked from sleep. 'What?' Then he said, 'No'.

'You going to say no, Cyrus, without thinking. You going to say no? What they going to do here in Manzanilla? Catch fish in the sea?'

'They have land. They have a house here.'

'And for how many is this mansion?'

'What?' For she had never talked so to him before, never raised her voice above a supplicating meekness. 'Rose!'

'I ain't no rose again, Cyrus. I ain't no rose. Look at me! This skin and bones ain't no rose. Let the children go.'

'Go? And didn't Lorna go? Didn't Lorna go?'

' Yes, Lorna went, and married and have children.'

'Married? You call that skufflin' little fella a husband? Driftin' around, can't settle down, can't mind his children. That is the married that Lorna married?'

'Is Lorna life. You can't make life for people; they have to live it for theyself. And she is not the first – '

'And she won't be the last of your children to throw away their life if your foolishness prevail.'

'They going, Cyrus. They going. I going to tell them to go. Do what you want. You live your life already, and I live it here with you. Okay. But I telling them to go. They can't breathe in this place.'

'They will breathe well in Port of Spain. You better go with them: you will breathe well too.'

He worked it all into the latticework of this dragon, into the scales and the threads, the exodus then of his grand-mother and his two unmarried aunts from Manzanilla, leaving the tall immortelle and the dying bananas and the cocoa trees with pods small as grains of pigeon peas, and the old road and the old man (and he, thinking: Who will varnish the tables? Who will polish the floor?), unyielding to the last, as if he knew that whatever route they took their fate would be worse than to keep faith with a promise that he could not, if he were sane, expect still to be honoured. He worked it all in: they, his grandmother and young aunts, leaving for a house in St James; he, back to his mother rocking the last baby to sleep and waiting for his father, Sam Prospect, the miracle man, who she was crazy enough to go with when he left the cocoa estate in Manza-nilla to go to Port of Spain, without money or schooling or trade, filled with that sense of escape and that idea of his manness which had no chance to flower under the foreman, among labourers and cocoa and immortelle, and which would not find it easier in the city where he went from job to job, giving one up for another after a month or two, or maybe it was fired, working longest as a barman in a

rum shop, fathering five children and ever so often dis-
appearing, leaving the children and their mother waiting:
she, sending little notes by Aldrick to his aunts and grandmother: 'Send a little money, send a little sugar, until Sam
come home,' and when Sam did not come home, leaving
the eldest boy to take care of the smaller ones, going out to
work, washing and cleaning, a maid in white people
kitchen; then at last Sam suddenly reappearing with long
hurried strides as if he had just stepped out to the corner
and was returning to go out again, hollow-eyed from
nights gambling, coming home with a big brown paper bag
with groceries and presents for the children; and his
mother, who had prayed so often and long for his returning, going down on her knees on the floor of hardened
mud in the Spiritual Baptist church up on Laventille where
God came down every Wednesday night if the police didn't
get there before Him, now that he had come, saying not a
word, not even crying. He would hear them in the kitchen,
his father pleading, saying, Hush, Lorna, hush; and his
mother not saying a word, and he, Sam, promising again to
get a good job and settle down and see about her and the
children; and then his mother finally saying, between the
crackling of the paper as she took the groceries out the bag,
in a voice that threatened to rise from its whispering into a
scream: Don't, Sam. Don't promise anything. Just go as
you going. Don't promise anything. And his father saying,
softly, with tears in his voice, Hush, hush, hush – he
must have been holding her in his arms and rocking her
like a baby, saying, hush, hush, hush: for the paper would
be no longer crackling.

Oh, the miracle of their surviving: the miracle of his
mother bringing up five children and waiting, waiting, for
Sam, the miracle man, always moving with that busy
speed, always on the look out for a better break, a better
job, a chance, trying to the very end of his days to be the
man he had left Manzanilla to become, so that when the
crane fell on his back and broke it, down on the wharves

where he had been working off and on for two weeks, they had to take his hands out his pockets.

Maybe that was his gift to his children, this sense of miracle and manness, this surviving on nothing and standing up still on your own two feet to be counted as somebody in a world where people were people, were human, by the amount of their property. Or, maybe it was not something acquired by him (Sam Prospect) but an ancestral gift handed down to generations of Prospects and later inherited by Aldrick; for when his mother died not too long after, and Aldrick and the rest of the children scattered across the face of the country, each one taken in by one relative or another, he would encounter this same sense of miracle and manness in his father's brother, Freddie, Uncle Freddie into whose care he was entrusted; Uncle Freddie from whom he learnt to make dragon; Uncle Freddie cooler than water and smoother, having the run of the city in a way his brother Sam never did, knowing at his age that it was wasteful to hurry, not wasting a gesture, saying to Aldrick the only words that he, Aldrick, could remember even now as his most often, no, his only lecture: 'Take it easy!' Take it easy: the words with which he answered every salutation and made every promise and consoled everyone. Take it easy, worked now into his dragon and its growing story of lives of miracle and manness and faith.

Working there now, thoughts of Sylvia kept nagging at his brain. Suddenly, since the night he had surprised her going to meet Guy, she had refused to leave his mind; and now, every time he turned he would see her flitting by or standing in that long soft sullen pose, her eyes and spirit and provoking limbs piercing and surrounding and entangling him like Shango drums that he was already fated to dance to; and he tried to puzzle out in his mind: how come he had managed to escape her before. Then, yesterday evening as he worked on his dragon costume, she had appeared before his open door, with high heeled shoes a size too big on, and one of those dresses that used to be fashionable seven years before, a white dress with no band at the waist, a bow at the back, three-quarter length sleeves, and long down to just below her knees, an ancient, almost bridal dress that someone, some aunt or cousin had handed over to her mother who had passed it on to her. She had appeared at the doorway of his little room in this outlandish costume, with red lipstick on her mouth, and her hair combed back and brushed up to a point at the back of her head and held together by a length of white ribbon, and stood there looking at him sew scales into the cloth of the dragon, stood there with a warm virginal softness and trembling about her, as if she had come both to give herself and to resist his taking her.

'You see I ain't have no space even to invite you in,' he had said, with a little half nervous laugh that was kinda new for him, indicating with a sweep of one hand the cluttered room with scattered pieces of cloth and tins of paint and scraps of tin, all the time aware of her white dress and red lipstick and high heeled shoes slack around her feet.

She had grinned back, softly too, half frightened, it seemed, waiting with that warm waiting that suggested the reaffirmation of an intimacy that she felt that their meeting a few nights before had created between them, waiting as if she expected from him a question to which she already had the answer, holding herself at arm's length away, watching as he worked the needle through the cloth of his costume.

'You like how it coming?' He lifted his head to say that, holding up for her gaze the section of the costume he was sewing.

'I ain't get my costume yet,' she said, as if she could wait no longer for the question she had stood there expecting.

He heard the words. He wanted to look at her; instead, he watched his needle and sewed, his mind tumbling, wanting to ask her the questions that were already tumbling in his head: You mean . . . ? You didn't? Guy didn't?

'I ain't get my costume yet,' she said again, her voice firmer now, containing neither triumph nor pride nor the joy that might have bubbled in it if his question had come first.

What he heard was the challenge and promise in her remark, the same challenge and promise that had resided in her person all these last years, that he had tried so hard to ignore, that he had successfully managed to ignore until she brought it to his door a few nights before; and she was bringing it again, hurling it at him now, with all the fragile softness and youth and warmth of her womanness, announced and emphasized and shouted out in the pathos and beauty and ridiculousness of the handed down dress and the oversized shoes and the lipstick and the ribbon in her hair.

He would not escape her this time. He was doomed: this came to his mind after she left – and she had waited the eternity at his door for some word from him, some sign that he understood, at least acknowledged what her words were saying. She had waited the eternity during which he continued to sew scales on to the costume, refusing even to think of her meaning, far more comment on it, thinking to try to smile, to make some joke, thinking to find some hole to escape through, knowing that for his manness sake the smile nor the joke wouldn't do. He couldn't let this girl come and stand before his door and be more woman than he was man. He couldn't let her come with that virginal and bridal and lady-like dignity and hope, that not only concerned him – indeed, went beyond being a challenge to him, was a statement of her promise to living, to her own hopes – and make a joke of it.

You is a princess, girl. You don't need those clothes and that lipstick, you is a princess just as you is everyday: the words came to his lips to say, but to say even that now, as hollow as it might have sounded, would not be a compliment; it would be a proposal. He couldn't do that. And he knew that it was not just the matter of buying her a costume either – not that he had the money even for that – but to make even that offer now was to begin to contradict the very guts and fibre of his own living: Aldrick was a dragon. He was a hustler, working nowhere; and the only responsibility he was prepared to bear now was to his dragon, that presentation on Carnival day of the self that he had lived the whole year. He had his life.

'Sylvia . . .' And as he raised his head he could see her alive eyes, eager, burning, shielding that invitation and promise, that woman-softness that was more prophecy than warning that she had the power to draw him into that world of ordinary living and caring that he had avoided all his life. 'Sylvia . . .' He knew he had to say something now. What, he didn't know even as he was preparing to say it. Then, mercifully, he heard Philo calling out his name. He turned to the sound. 'Haii!' he cried to the approaching Philo, 'Haii!'

She did not blink. Even as Philo approached she had stood there, her eyes fastened on Aldrick, as if she still had enough patience and strength and faith to wait on him, the stubborn wilfulness and truth to not be the one to surrender or default, enduring in the fifteen or twenty seconds it took Philo to cross the yard to Aldrick's place, the silence that was not of her making – she had said her piece – waiting still for Aldrick to complete whatever it was he had begun when he said her name; and she would not move even when Philo come up and turned to her, feigning surprise: 'Haii! That is you, Sylvia? No, that is not you.' Not even when he stepped up to her an arm's length away and let his muscled eyes rove over her in inspection from head to toe. Even when he reached out to put his hand on her in that friendly sensual way some men try to touch a beauty which they cannot otherwise embrace, she did not move: as she felt his touch, she slapped his face. It was only then that she turned and walked away.

'Sylvia!' Aldrick cried; and maybe the word might have died in his brain, or maybe he had suddenly gone deaf; he didn't hear a sound. He watched her walking away with that tall chaste insolent and disdaining tread, her head in the air, dragging her feet a little to keep the shoes from slipping off her feet.

'What wrong with her?' Philo had asked.

' You asking *me*?' But even as he said so he was thinking that Philo's coming had not rescued him at all. It had merely postponed the questions he had to face from not so much Sylvia as from himself; so that long after Philo left – and he had remained only a short time, holding his face where she had slapped him, and asking over and over again: 'What wrong with her?' – he was still thinking: I ain't get my costume yet, the words, which he had earlier failed to acknowledge, bouncing and flipping in his brain, turning him to their promise, to their challenge, causing in him a feeling of guilt, a sensation that he was alarmed and surprised that he could still feel.

'Haii! But what the hell I here worrying myself about?' he cried, when he came to himself and found himself seated at the edge of his bed, darkness gathering, the lamp not yet lit, and the boy still there. 'I ain't responsible for her. All I do is just see this girl going one night to meet a man; that is all. I don't even know if she went and meet him. I don't even know what under her dress. Haii!' He laughed aloud. 'Aldrick, you growing old, boy. You getting soft . . . And you.' He turned to the boy. 'It nearly dark, you ain't going home?' even then searching for a match to light the lamp, not looking at the boy.

'I leaving home,' the boy said.

He laughed, his back still turned to the boy. 'Don't make that kinda joke with me. Not today. You leaving home? What you leaving home for?' He turned now from the lamp he had lighted and saw the boy's face, and his own tone changed. He said softly, 'What you leaving home for?'

'He beat me again. Everytime he get drunk he beat me.

He beat everybody in the house.' The boy was crying.

'Who . . . ?' And now to his surprise, Aldrick realized that after two Carnivals, two years of the boy coming to his place and working with him, all he knew of him was his first name. He sat down on his bed, and his voice came squeaking out his belly: 'Who? Who is that beating you and everybody? Your father?'

'He ain't my father. He living with my mother. Fisheye.'

'Fisheye is your step-father?'

' You know him?'

Aldrick did know Fisheye. This knowledge made him cautious. 'Well, maybe you do something wrong. Maybe you don't learn your lessons or something. I used to get licks for that too, and I never leave home.'

' You don't know him when he drunk. My big brother Leroy: he beat Leroy so bad he break Leroy hand, and when they was carrying Leroy to hospital he tell my mother to tell the doctor that Leroy fall down from a tree, else he going to break her hand too.'

'He really don't make fun,' Aldrick said. 'But I . . . I not going to encourage you to run away. Where you will go? You have anybody near by where you could stay? 'cause I . . . you can't stay here, you know. You see how small this place is.'

Aldrick saw the boy's eyes filling again.

'Is not that I don't want you here, man; but, look at the size of this place.' And all the time thinking: two years, and I don't know the boy full name or where he living or who his mother is or anything. Look at that, eh! And, *I ain't get my costume yet* flashed across his brain. 'Look, this ain't my business, you know,' he said, with a kind of softness and aggravation. 'This is between you and you step-father. I serious. I mean, this is family business. I don't know anything about it. I mean, I don't know what it is between you and your mother and Fisheye. You understand?'

The boy said nothing, and Aldrick fell silent, waiting for the boy to understand and to leave, and when he saw that the boy was not going to leave without his urging, he said: 'Okay, wipe your face and go. I can't do nothing. This is family business. You have to understand that.'

The boy left then, backing out of the door, dragging his feet, his eyes overflowing.

'Fisheye is a hell of a man,' Aldrick said aloud. Then he lit a cigarette and went to the door. 'Wha—!' The boy was still there. Aldrick began to tell him again that it was family business, that his own place was too small, and so on, when he remembered that the boy had heard all that before.

'Okay,' Aldrick said, 'okay. Come, let's go. I going to carry you home. Come. It ain't my business, you know, but I going to have a talk with him anyway.'

Aldrick went inside and slipped on his shoes. He didn't know where this softness was coming from. Maybe he was getting old in truth. 'Come,' he said to the boy when he was ready, strengthening his resolve; for, on Calvary Hill Fisheye was a man whose business even the police were reluctant to meddle in.

4   The Bad John

He never liked the name Fisheye. In Moruga they would never have thought to give him such a name, for he already had a name they knew, a name started long before he was born in his grandfather, Otway John, whose father came direct from Africa, black and smooth like the underside of a tannia leaf on a dark night, and continued in his father, Samuel, a Baptist preacher who, when he raised his voice to preach, was heard in every corner of Moruga, and in his brothers, Samuel's sons, Clarence and Isidore and Dudley and Findlay and Silbert and Carlton, tall strong men who could handle their fists, and were good, each one of them, with a stick, since their father, before he became a preacher, was a champion stickfighter who had himself schooled each one of them in the art of stickfighting; so that in Moruga they were a fearsome band, and for all their bulging eyes, no one would have dared call them any name more derogatory than John.

But when he came to Port of Spain they didn't ask him his name; they gave him one. 'My name is Belasco . . . Belasco John,' he used to tell them, but they refused to hear him; so he fought them over it. That was how they knew he could fight, that was how they knew he was brave; though they would have found that out anyway, for when he came to Port of Spain to live just after the war, he was, at eighteen, already too young, too strong, too eager to prove himself a man to have escaped the violence in which men were tried and tested in that town.

Before he got the room on Calvary Hill, he was staying at Lefthander, a fellar from Moruga, in a little room on Charlotte Street where Lefthander had a woman living-with, making a child for him. That time he was working on Marine Square as a truck loader for Laidlow Brothers, and working real hard too, not only because Lefthander wasn't working nowhere and had this woman making a child for him to see about, but to celebrate the strength he felt in his arms, to show Port of Spain what Moruga could do. In those first few months he loaded trucks, lifted bags, pushed and pulled crates until his body throbbed with a wonderful pain; and sometimes, he used to pause and lick the sweat flowing down his face from off the corners of his lips and taste it in his mouth, and look at the muscles on his arms and feel the strength in him – not even that he was young, he didn't even think that yet – and he would look across at the other fellars to see how they were working, eyeing their muscles, comparing theirs to his, measuring the amount of sweat they sweated, and feeling kinda like he was a man, kinda like he was tall and wide and big; and it didn't worry him at all that they were getting a bigger pay.

'Boy, you's a devil for work,' they used to look at him and say. 'Jeez-us!' And it was only long afterwards, after he had fought Ajax, who wasn't no real foreman, who was just working there longer than the other loaders and had this big chest and gruff voice and cussed louder than anybody, and none of the bosses telling him anything; it was only after that fight, when he made a few friends, that he learnt from Lonie that they had been deliberately leaving all the work to him. 'Well, we see like you feel you could kill work,' Lonie reported, 'so we say "okay, go ahead," to see if work really going to dead.'

In a way he wished that Lonie hadn't told him anything, that he had gone on working like a fool, watching his muscles grow, tasting the sweat off his face; for now that he had this wisdom he couldn't be a fool again, and without being that kinda fool there was nothing to do with himself.

He had gotten the room on Calvary Hill then, and didn't even have Lefthander and the girl who was making a baby to talk to. He didn't know what it was in his head. At nights he couldn't sleep, lay awake tossing, feeling a sense of use-lessness, feeling as if he was here, and life, real life, was in some region far away from him, and to make sure that he was himself he would have to get up and go and burst a man head.

'Is the devil,' Lonie told him. 'Same thing uses to happen to me before I had this girl I now living with. You have to get a girl or some kinda thing to get you so tired that you can't think.'

He smiled.

'I telling you, man,' Lonie insisted. 'You have to find something to do with yourself, else the devil going to stay in your head. Why you don't play some football?'

'It will go away,' he said, because he wanted to appear in charge of himself, and anyway, football wasn't his game.

He began to go to the cinema. Every night almost, he went to Royal or Empire, whichever was showing a western double; and after the show, walking home up the Hill, the picture fresh in his mind, walking kinda slow, he would feel for a few moments his strength, his youth, his promise fill him, and he would walk, the fastest gun alive, his long hands stiff at his sides, his fingers ready to go for the guns he imagined holstered low on his hips. But no one wanted to draw against him; and he would pick his way between the garbage and dog shit with his secret power and invisible guns, his eyes searching the shadows for a hidden gunman – in which movie was it that someone had said: 'Every shadow is a gunman?' – but all he saw was maybe a few fellars gambling under the street light, or a man and his woman quarrelling. Back in his room, he felt crushed by his own strength, spun by the quickness in him. Now and again he would punch the boards of the partition, and he would overhear his neighbour's resigned comment: 'The devil in there with that boy.' The devil remained with him.

He began to develop a crawl, a way of walking that was kinda dragging and slow, in which his knees barely bent, his feet were kept close and his legs spread apart to give the appearance of being bow-legged from riding a horse. He walked, crawled to and from work, to and from the cinema, tall, slow, a bow-legged cowboy, with his hair combed up on his head in a big muff, his shirt pushed into his pants resting low on his waist, his hands hanging loose and empty at his sides; that and the cut of his head, his bulging eyes, and the soft sullenness of his lips issuing a challenge, just waiting for a man to snicker or say a rough word to him so he could cuff him down; but, his readiness was its own warning, and he went, almost a spectacle, unmolested through the streets, nobody wanting to tackle him.

One day, eating a bread and shark in a Port of Spain parlour, he suddenly decided not to pay for it.

'I ain't paying,' he said when the proprietor, seeing him get up to leave, asked him for money.

'You ain't what?' It was a little place run by this old, partly paralyzed fellow and his wife. And the old man, vexed by the tone of insolence and insult in his person and voice, forgot his own age and condition and began to move around the counter towards him. 'You not what? You crazy or something?'

And he had, without panic, stood his ground and watched the old man coming towards him, feeling very tall and very much a bandit like in a western movie – and the people in the place watching like in a western too. But the wife held the old man back. 'No, Donald. Don't put yourself in trouble for a bread and shark,' and, turning to him: 'Go on, Sonny, take it. Go!' And back to her husband: 'You don't know the devil everywhere? Leave him. He will get what he lookin' for.'

'Go on, Sonny,' she said to him, and he had stood there, stupid all of a sudden, and he pushed his hands into his pockets, and he wanted to pay, but he didn't know how to cross the ten or so feet that separated him from the counter.

'A knife!' somebody cried out. 'Is a knife in his pocket.' And people began to scamper, and he saw the old woman's sad eyes, and he heard her pleading: 'Go on, Sonny. Don't look for trouble. You done eat the bread and shark already. Go on.'

And he stood there, very silly, not knowing how to pay the money and not knowing how to leave and go; there was no triumph in either now. He tried to smile to make the old woman feel more comfortable. And he was still standing there with this stupid smile on his face and his hands in his pockets when two policemen came in, followed by a band of spectators who wanted to see the excitement.

Somebody shouted: 'He have a knife!'

And while he was there standing, with this silly smile on his face, trying to take his hands out his pockets to show that he was unarmed, he saw the policemen in front of him, saw a baton coming at his head. He moved, slipped inside it, held it. Then he knew he had this baton in his hand and he saw one policeman fall and he heard the people screaming and he heard a police whistle blasting, and he had this baton in his hand, and before he could decide what to do with it, for the two policemen were on the ground, he saw a whole crowd of grey-shirted policemen coming towards him, a whole army of them, like in *Guns Across the River*, and he was standing there with the baton in his hand swinging, and he tasted blood in his mouth, and then he was floating down very slow, falling down very slow, like he had all the time in the world to fall, and it would be the last thing he would do, forever and forever fall.

'Six months' hard labour!' the magistrate said. 'Jail is the only thing to straighten out you young hooligans.'

THE BAD JOHN 53

And not knowing what else to do, he had shrugged his shoulders and curled his lips and showed his teeth in a tough smile, and strolled off to the cell ahead of the police guards.

All jail did was teach him time. What it did was take away whatever remained of urgency or hurry from his movements. He took his time: to comb his muff, to fold the sleeves of his long-sleeved shirt just above the wrist, to compose his gestures; now, when he opened his arms, the gesture contained all the careful tension of a man playing an accordion.

It was with the same tense slowness that he walked, crawled the streets of Port of Spain when he came out of prison, wearing his six months' hard labour and the knowledge that he alone for almost half an hour had battled more than a dozen policemen as a string of medallions pinned on the chest of an old soldier from the West India Regiment on Remembrance Day, believing that everybody knew of his exploits; but no change came to his life. He could feel himself wasting, marking time, the strength in his arms and the quickness in him that he tried to throw off balance in his crawl, flowing up against his thighs, pressing against his armpits, his own strength stifling him. He wanted to burst out of himself, to fly out and become himself. He walked into one club after another, seeking the battle that would free him; but all he met with were old bad Johns, warriors who had seen their time and lived now on their fame, their very names forgotten by everyone outside a small circle of acquaintances, and some younger fellars, mediocre men who had no class nor name and who would acquire neither, were satisfied to live out their promise in sullen corners of night clubs, at the side of some whore they owned, brandishing a knife or a razor they claimed they could use. He was too strong, too swift, too gifted for them; and he would hurl them back, two, three, four at a time, without even rumpling the tall muff in his hair. In jail, Reds, a fellow from Calvary Hill steelband, had encouraged him to come and join the band; and, although he had thought of it off and on since coming out of prison, he had put off checking out the band until some time had passed because he didn't want to give the impression that he was all that lonely and anxious for friends. One day, he walked up the Hill and joined the band.

For all the years he remained in Calvary Hill steelband, he never became a real steelbandsman, a musician. The only instrument that he ever learned to play was the three-note boom, a massive three foot steel drum carried in those days before the improvements, before the canopied trucks and trailers and pans mounted on stands with wheels, by the strongest man in the band; and he could beat iron, those lengths of steel that rang out above the lower notes of the drums, ringing out a challenging, pulsating rhythm, chiming the battle cry. From the first, he was a warrior, a fighter, entering bodily into the violence boiling in the guts of the city; and soon everyone on Calvary Hill would know his name – for those were the days when every district around Port of Spain was its own island, and the steelband within its boundaries was its army, providing warriors to uphold its sovereignty. Those were the war days, when every street corner was a garrison; and to be safe, if you came from Belmont, you didn't let night catch you in St James; if your home was Gonzales Place, you didn't go up Laventille; and if you lived in Morvant, you passed San Juan straight.

In this war, in this army, Fisheye at last found the place where he could be a man, where his strength and quickness had meaning and he could feel pride in belonging and purpose to his living, and where he had all the battles he had dreamed of, and more, to fight. While he was with them, Calvary Hill became a name to be respected, began to be spoken of with the same measure of awe with which young men whispered Desperadoes, Rising Sun, Renegades, Red Army, Hell Yard, Tokyo – bands that announced and advertised in their very names the fact and dreams of a violence they cultivated all year round, in constant battles fought between themselves, with razors, knives, in hand to hand combat, in night clubs, gambling houses and on street corners, vaulting often into more embracing wars in which warriors from one band, armed with cutlasses, sticks, big stones, and that most fearsome creation forged in the arsenal of the combating armies – the iron bolt – would invade the other's territory, attacking whosoever they found out of doors at the time. Calvary Hill became one of the tall names, joining with others to turn Carnival days to the celebration of their warriorhood, plunging into Port of Spain, costumed in warriors' robes, celebrating and invoking and lifting to god-hood, Ghengis Khan and Attila and Spartacus, Alexander, Hitler, Conquistadors, bandits, US Marines, making the city their arena, their savannah, their stage, parading, bragging their might, warming, stretching their limbs in the tough, hot, rejoicing steelband music their accompanying bands, after months of practising, had captured to exalt them, to lift them into their warriorhood, often getting giddy, drunk, with their power before the sun went down, unveiling their armament: their cutlasses and razors and iron bolts and bottles and stones, making the city their own, sending women looking on in a panic to secure their children and scamper home, the whole becoming a ballet of wailing children, scampering silent people, screaming ambulances and helmeted policemen rushing to and fro, more in a gesture at peace-keeping than with any serious intent to stem the thrust of the affirming warriors. Fisheye delighted in this living; and soon, his name had been added to the roster of heroes that ruled Port of Spain: Batman, Big Sax, Mastifay, Tom Keen, Zigilee, Baron and Barker.

When he first joined the band he had bought a black hat with a silver band. He wanted the hat to be sorta like a trade mark. He kinda hoped that fellars would start calling him

Black Hat instead of Fisheye; but Fisheye remained his name. He wore the hat anyway; and for years in his heyday, he would be recognized on Carnival days, moving along the lines of Calvary Hill steelband, by his black hat, its silver band gleaming, his shirt unbuttoned down his chest, his long arms lifted above his head in that tall gesture of salutation and waiting, accepting on behalf of himself and his fellow warriors the acclaim of the band's supporters, signalling his confidence and readiness for battle. One time in a fight with Tokyo, a fellow named Cat stuck a knife right through the hat. Fisheye didn't get hurt, and although he had felled Cat with a flying butt, it didn't recompense. He liked the hat. Afterwards, he kinda rounded out the knife marks into holes, and he wore the hat now with a special pride. Sometimes, to impress young fellars just coming into the band, he would take off his hat and point to the holes and say: 'You see where a fellar shoot me!' In a way he was sorry that they hadn't been real bullet holes, like in a western.

Those were glorious days for him. He had a girl, Yvonne, who was a limbo dancer in Miramar, living with him, and they had some real good times, real good times. Sometimes they would take the train from Port of Spain and go to Flanagin Town or Brasso, or ride right down to the end of the line, Rio Claro, for nothing really, just to be with one another and to watch the people come on and go off, and the crowds gathered at those country stations who assembled there for the same reason, to watch who was coming in and who was going out, and then they would take a bus and go to the beach at Mayaro. He remembered those times easiest now, and how it felt nice to be alive and to have your own girl and Reds have his girl and Terry his, and they all sit down over a bottle, just talking or playing all fours for water – losers drink – or just off by himself, he and Yvonne, sitting under a coconut tree like a tourist, with his feet in the water and the waves washing them sometimes, and Yvonne talking about things, the world, because she was an intelligent girl (she went to high school and was from a good family too) and he listening. She had a nice shape and fellars would pass and watch her, not for long, for he was sitting there, but long enough for her to know that she was admired; and things was so right between them that it didn't even worry him; she was his woman, and the two of them was so much in tune that sometimes they didn't even have to talk to know thoughts in each other's head. When he saw a joke in something, you could bet she would see the same joke too, and they would just watch each other and smile without even saying a word. And lucky! He was so lucky in gambling that one month he gave her four hundred dollars. 'Go and shop,' he told her. And she went and bought all kinda nice things, things for the house, and a shaving set and bottle of after-shave cologne for him, that he didn't want to use because a man not supposed to smell so. That was his season, those years: the baddest man in town respecting him, and everywhere he pass on the Hill, people calling out to him, not because they were afraid of him, but out of a warm embracing brotherhood and comradeship. Girls wanted to be his woman, schoolboys were pointing him out to their friends: 'That is Fisheye! That is Fisheye!' saying, 'Right-o Fisheye!' and he saying, 'Right-o, how it going?' And if he liked their looks, sometimes giving them six cents to go in the parlour and buy something.

It was a wonderful thing, Calvary Hill steelband, and he was at the centre of it; belonging to it and it to him. He watched it growing: schoolboys from the Hill drawn to the music, discerning in it the repository of their warriorhood and living, had begun to flow into the steelband tent, even fellars going to college, unable to resist the call, the shout to the warrior in them, that no latin or math or the promise of respectability had quelled, were beginning to slide in, quietly, some of them, so their parents wouldn't know, so their teachers wouldn't see them; some came bold, put out of their homes by parents who said. I don't want no hooligan in this house,' going to live at another relative who maybe understood a little better the magic tug of the steelband. Fisheye delighted in it, delighted in the place and the people, the growing girls and the old women and the old fellars with fire in their eyes, watching for something; but mostly, he was drawn to the young fellars, the fidgety young fellars with serious faces and a slow crawl, fellars who wanted to explode the strength and quickness in them. And they were drawn to him, not out of his fame alone, but to the fire in him, the light; and he was rough and tough and gentle with them, and they would talk about battles, make jokes, and he would advise them about women, the world, their youth and promise, talking like a brother to them. And sometimes, not often, one of the fellars would meet him alone and say: 'Fish, I glad you had that talk with me the other day. I think I on the right track now.' And he would say, 'That ain't nutten, man,' but his voice would be sticking in his throat, and water would be right behind his eyes, so keenly did such things touch him.

But, with all this love and power, he made no move to go beyond living his warriorhood; and he went into battle after battle with that dull, triumphing might, until that night after the fight with Desperadoes. A lot of fellars got cut in that fight, and Yvonne's cousin, who was a Desperadoes, got seventeen stitches down his back from a cutlass wound.

'Suppose all-you did kill him, Belasco.'

'Is war, Yvonne. It coulda been me get cut.'

'But why you have to fight one another?'

He didn't understand that one. It wasn't that he had any personal grudge against Desperadoes. The two bands, Desperadoes and Calvary Hill, existing not more than a mile from each other, peopling different sections of the same slum that ringed this side of the city, two peaks on the same rebelling Hill, had been for years locked in a war that

they themselves must have created out of their own need to
cultivate and uphold that spirit of rebellion and warriorhood, splitting what must have once been one tribe in that
cause more holy and essential than brotherhood for their
human hopes and surviving. In fact, to Fisheye, their
warring had become the celebration and consecration of a
greater brotherhood – a love that gained its nurture in the
fierceness of their warring.

'Who we will fight then? Is war, Yvonne.'

And he remembered how he had laughed quickly to
escape the puzzling thing that was hidden somewhere in
all this happening, and pulled her to him in bed; but she
had pulled back: 'You mean you will go on fighting one
another? Why you can't join up?'

'And fight who?'

'Fight the people who keeping down black people. Fight
the government.'

At first it did not register what she was suggesting, for
the truth was that he wanted nothing but to live, to be, to
be somebody for people to recognize, so when they see him
they would say: 'That is Fisheye!' and give him his space;
and when they see someone who concerned him, to say:
'That is Fisheye woman! That is Fisheye friend,' and not to
fuck around either of them to make him turn beast. He
didn't think about the government or about black people or
anything. He didn't think of the steelband as an army to
fight any other battle but those it fought against other steelbands. He didn't think of anything. But as soon as Yvonne
said it, he saw it: these steelbands could be one army. He,
Fisheye, could be a general in it.

'You know you talking sense,' he said to her. 'You know
you *really* talking sense.'

'We have to sign peace with the bands,' he told Reds
right after. 'We is all one army – Desperadoes, Invaders,
Tokyo, Casablanca, Rising Sun: all o' we is one. We's the
same people catching hell.'

'Make peace, and do what?' Reds asked.

'Fight. Fight the people that keeping us down. Take over the government.'

'Take over the government?' Reds laughed. He said: ' You will be the premier. Fisheye, you crazy!'

'This man crazy,' he told Terry and some fellars from the band. 'He want to make peace with the bands – and that ain't all. He want us to take over the government. He going to be premier.'

The fellars laughed too. They started to call him The Premier.

'Premier, I want a job for my brother. Premier, help me get a house for my sister,' they teased. It kinda surprised him, this attitude of, particularly, Terry and Reds. He used to think of them as bigger men, as fellars with ideas, fellars with sense in their heads. They kinda surprised him. But he suffered himself to be teased by them, to be the butt of their jokes, refusing to relent, to give in, to reduce his vision to the joke they insisted that it become. He watched them laugh. But their laughter only revealed to him the limits that they had set on their warriorhood. So that long afterwards when, no longer in the band, he would be standing on the street corner, one foot on the wall and a matchstick between his teeth, among new friends, young rebels of a new generation, he would say of Terry and Reds: 'They just wanted to be bad Johns. Me, I was a general all the time.'

But he didn't know it then with enough certainty. He thought it was the craziness again, the devil coming back into his head, cramping him, making him feel in need of air, of space, of wings. Battles with Renegades and Desperadoes that used to be such a thrill now left him empty, like nothing.

'Leave the band, Belasco,' Yvonne advised him. 'Leave it.'

But leave and go where? Leave and do what? She could never understand, nor could he explain, that the band was life to him. It was not a question of his wanting an

alternative – the steelband was his life. It wasn't something that he could just ups and leave.

Then, just like that, the bands signed peace. No. They
did not sign peace, peace overtook them; and though a
great fuss was made in the newspapers about this peace,
with men from Calvary Hill and Desperadoes shaking
hands and Inspector Rose from Besson Street Police
Station standing with his two hands round the shoulders of
Terry and Little John from Desperadoes, the war between
them had ended long before. Fellars really didn't want to
fight each other any more. The bad John, the warrior, had
lost zest for the fratricidal war.

'Good!' Fisheye thought. 'Good!' For he felt that the
peace would bring, would begin, cooperation, that fellars
would come together; and, that coming together, they
would see their strength, see their potential.

But this peace was no furtherance of his dream. It was a
pleasant peace, a nice peace, a peace of ending rather than
of beginning. It didn't cause the bands to turn their eyes
away from each other outwards to the world beyond the pan
yards and street corners, beyond the haunts of steelbandsmen to a larger arena, a bigger world, a world with a more
comprehensive reality, where resided the levers of power
that moved people, that moved them. It was as if they were
purposely blind to this world, as if they believed that their
gestures were only relevant when directed at each other,
that meaning for them was anchored in the world of the
steelband and of the street corner. So that the peace did not
join them or move them, it merely ended the nature of the
violence between them.

The steelband tent became a concert hall. Where fellars
had talked about battles, they talked now about music.
Fellars would come into the tent and stand silent before
the drums, their heads cocked to one side, their faces
frowning as they strained to listen for some note, some
note that the band had the gift to deliver and they to savour.
Battles on Carnival days between rival warriors became

contests of skill between competing orchestras, warriors became critics of music, the advertisers and upholders of the musical genius of the bands to which they belonged. Reds and Terry arguing with Man Man and Little John about whether it is Desperadoes or Calvary Hill playing the best Liebestraum.

Fisheye watched for it to go beyond this. He watched for the bands, the warriors to come together to do something, to make some dent in the real world. And for years he walked the lines of his band on Carnival days, with his black hat with the bullet holes he had cut in it, his face unsmiling, his shirt unbuttoned down his chest, his unclenched hands lifted above his head in that gesture of triumph and acknowledgement, trying singly to summon into the presence of this masquerade, ideas, feelings, memories of warriorhood back again, so much so that Terry and Reds felt moved to tell him: 'Take it easy, man. Enjoy yourself. We ain't expecting no war; we in peace with Desperadoes.'

But on Carnival days, in the heat, with rum flowing and drums booming and people filling the streets, the blood would rush to his head, and the warrior would rear in him again, and he would go to the front of the band and take the flag and wave it, wave it with all that old violence and challenge, clearing a path through spectators, and sometimes moving through whatever band was approaching in the opposite direction on the narrow street, in that gesture of provocation and insult that, even with peace, strained the restraint of every but the weakest band.

'No, man. No, man,' Terry and Reds would tell him. 'We don't want that.'

They assigned members of the band to keep an eye on him so that they could quickly surround him and prevent him plunging the band into a conflict they had no desire to enter. But sometimes he would turn upon his very guards and battle them. People said he was *mounted*: a spirit of a warrior was inside him, and he couldn't help himself. At certain times he just *had* to fight.

He thought the chance had come for the bands to join together and battle for something, when he saw the new bands coming on to the streets for Carnival. These bands were the white bands: well-off, light-skinned boys from prosperous families and good schools, fellars who in all the years of violence and struggle had had nothing to do with them, now, in the lull of this peace that had spread throughout the bands, were beginning to come out in their own steelbands whose very names – Merry Boys, Dixie Land, Star Land, Happy Boys, held no salute nor acknowledgement of the fire, the blood, the heat of the early days of the movement; they were coming now, Fisheye felt, as if they had a right to this peace, this easy passage. And, yes, they had this easy passage in everything else, in schools, in jobs, in positions; but this was his territory. This was slum, street corner territory; and it burned him to see them entering so casually.

'Run them outa town, Reds,' he said. 'Let them feel the heat. Bust their head. Let their blood run on Port of Spain streets.'

'Run them? Why?'

'Why?'

'Yes. Why? They helping to make steelband respectable . . . Us . . . we respectable.'

'You mean you want them to accept you, Reds. You want *them* to accept you?'

'Fisheye, you like too much fight,' Reds said.

'Yes,' he said. 'Yes, Reds, I like too much fight.'

All that year there was no peace in him. He was feeling not only the pain of his vision, but a new loneliness; and he had this sense of being betrayed by Terry and Reds and the whole warriorhood movement. He began to drink heavily, to go to clubs and drink rum and look for fights, trying to make of those he succeeded in provoking, a statement of his warriorhood; but there was nothing sacred nor noble about them: they were just brawls; but he continued to seek them, even with Yvonne begging him to stop, to change his ways, to turn to some other thing.

'If you don't do something with life, Belasco, life going to do something with you,' she warned. 'If you intend to spend all your days as a bad John, I could get a decent man.' And when he picked her up off the floor where his blow had sprawled her, and tried to comfort her and to explain, he could feel no yielding in her, and he knew that the end for them was not far away.

Even his luck changed. He was so unlucky gambling that he couldn't call a right bet in the club; and, for money, but also to assert himself that he wasn't slipping, that he was still Fisheye, one of the three top fighters in the city, he began to stand on the street corner, the gateway to the Hill, demanding money from newcomers or working men who were too timid to refuse him. But there at the corner of the street, he learnt anew that the people on the Hill respected him, that they still looked to him as guardian of their peace. It amazed and shamed him. Tears came to his eyes at this understanding: that in all this shit, people looked to him, respected him. Fellars would see him and just so call him for a beer, and say: 'Hold that,' and when he looked in his hands, he would see a dollar, two dollars, two shillings. Jesus Christ! And one day, walking through the market, going to buy something, this old lady, really old, with kinda smiling eyes under all her wrinkles, call him: 'Sonny, come!' and when he went to her, watchful, 'cause he didn't know her, she handed him a yam. 'Take this.'

'You sure is me you want to give this yam?' he asked her.

And she said, 'Ain't you the one they call Fisheye. I living up Calvary Hill.' And he took the yam and he bought a paper bag to put it in, and he walked home light and slow and thinking and vexed with Terry and Reds and glad to be in the world and loving people. And that was the day that

Yvonne chose to pack up her things and go. She wasn't there for him to tell her about the yam. He sat down on the edge of the bed – she had left the bed. She didn't take a thing, just left – and he wanted to cry, wished he could cry, but he didn't know how to.

For weeks he went nightly to Miramar to see if he would find her; but she had left the job, they said. But he kept on going from club to club in search of her. It was foolish, he knew. They said she had gone with a fellar active in the new political party, the PNM. But he felt as if he wanted to say something to her, maybe just see her; as if at least sight of her would bring the completion, the end of the relationship that she had withdrawn from. And maybe that was why he began to go to Woodford Square whenever the PNM was having a meeting. He hoped he would spot her. Maybe she would even be on the bandstand giving a speech; maybe he would catch a glimpse of her in the crowd. But the PNM was its own happening. Something like a religion, it was capturing people. Old women were bouncing. Muscles swelled on the arms of young men and a glint of battle was coming into their eyes. Fellars was talking. He couldn't understand the words. He doubted that they could explain them; but you really didn't need words to understand. You don't need words to understand the roaring of an ocean. Words were just a kind of background dressing, a kinda screen, a sound, the sounds. Manifesto, Nationhood, Culture, Colonialism. It was something to talk to Yvonne about. And alone, for he went to these meetings alone, like a wanted man in the midst of crowds, he could feel it; this was it. This was the thing that the steelband might have become, if fellars had sense, if they had vision. This was it, something joining people to people and people to dreams and dreams to hope that man would battle for more than to proclaim the strength of his arms, would lift their arms to break down these shanty towns and clean up the dog shit of the streets and the filth of gutters and build something clean, something tall. He wanted to enter it, to join it, become part of it, this wonderful thing that was going to fight colonialism, was going to stand up for the people, was going to create jobs and make us a nation. No. It was not talk. Thousands of people were there. He could see them, could feel them. It was a real thing. It wasn't a hustle to him. Or maybe it was that for all the years he had lived in the city, he was too countrified still, too given to dreams, too much swept along by hope, too great a believer in his own strength, in the possibility that he could, in company with men, make something happen.

He didn't officially join the PNM. He was suddenly shy and awkward before its compelling promise, before the important people running around with long words on the tips of their tongues. He was just a fighter. He just wanted you to point him to the enemy and say, 'Go!' He didn't even have a stick in his hand or a knife in his pocket. He was two eyes watching from the crowd, watching for the enemy to show himself, listening for the traitors to talk. One night he beat up five fellars for saying 'Fuck the PNM'. Now his gestures were beginning to flow again, his rhythm came back. He crawled through Woodford Square at the head of three fellars, with his belief like a halo around him, saying nothing, nothing at all, just watching, just waiting to fight. The elections came, the PNM won. No fight. He couldn't understand that. He couldn't understand what they had won. Maybe Yvonne might have been able to explain to him. She went to high school, she knew things. But white people were still in the banks and in the businesses along Frederick Street. The radio still spoke with a British voice. He couldn't understand.

'No, I can't understand this,' he told Reds. 'I don't see what we win.'

'You like too much fight, General Fisheye,' Reds told him.

And maybe he liked too much fight, in truth. Maybe life, real life, was not just fighting. Maybe you had to have brains, you had to have a manifesto and a programme; you had to go to college.

Maybe he was just crazy anyway. Maybe Reds was right. You had to know how to live. All politicians belong to the same society, and is only the people who fight.

Maybe he was too young, too innocent still. He didn't know. So when Reds came and asked him if he wanted a job on a government project – Crash Programme – they called it, he said okay.

'We support them. They must take care of us,' Reds explained. 'You don't have to work, just go on the job and give in your name.' So who was he? It was better than hustling two bobs from a working man. So he went to work on this job where they were building a concrete wall to hold up a landslide. He picked up a trowel to go and mix some cement. The boss called him in the office and told him he would be foreman, and he shrugged his shoulders and said all right.

On evenings he would go by the Corner, not to hustle anybody, just to watch, watch the people, see them walk, to say in his mind, 'this is my Hill, and these is my people,' and to wave at little fellars who called out to him, and sometimes to take a drink or offer one. He met this girl, Daphne, and though she had three children, she was a nice girl, and they moved in together. Things wasn't bad, and he thought maybe he could change. Maybe he could just try to be, to survive, without fighting anybody or wanting any position, or building anything, just going along, drifting along; and that Carnival was the only one he didn't get into a fight. The silver band on his black hat, frayed and aged, had finally dropped off. Without it and with the two bullet holes, the hat looked comical. He put it on and jumped into the band. He didn't get drunk that Carnival either. He was sweet the whole time, and smiling, watching the people; helping the little boys to push the trolleys upon which the steel drums were mounted, watching how importantly they did this, and with what pride.

This was their band. They belonged to it; it belonged to them.

And it was these little fellars he thought about when he saw that thing they called sponsorship coming into steel-band. At first it didn't worry him. He didn't even really notice it, because it started in one of the light-skinned bands – Merry Boys or Dixie Land or one of them. They came on the road that Carnival with Cicada Cigarettes printed on their jerseys and on their pans. It didn't worry him because he didn't consider them real bands. They had no real place, no community, no Hill where people was people and the band was a part of them, the band was their orchestra, to give them meaning; to sing them. So it didn't worry him that they came out with these cigarettes printed on their jerseys and their pans. People do all kinda crazy things, anyway; and they wasn't pushing anybody out of anything. They wasn't breaking up nothing. But when he saw Desperadoes the following year, that was something. For Desperadoes was the baddest band in the island, the band where the people was one. When they appeared on the road with new pans and emblem and waving a new flag: Sampoco Oil Company Gay Desperadoes, well, he nearly went out his head. Gay? *Gay* Desperadoes. That was the end. And instead of the little fellars pushing the pans, you had the sponsors: the sponsor's wife and the sponsor's daughter and the sponsor's friends, a whole section of them, their faces reddened by the excitement and the sun, smiling and jumping out of time, singing, All Ah We Is One.

Last year Casablanca and Rising Sun got their sponsors, and even Tokyo came on the streets wearing the colours of Matta and Matta, and with these strange people among them. Everybody friendly, everybody nice, everybody well behaved, and men like Harry and Tommy Gun and Slip-away grinning, and walking behind the band.

'Reds,' he said. 'Reds,' and he was serious this time. This time it was his own idea out his own head. 'Reds, I hope you-all ain't thinking about getting sponsor in this band.'

'How you mean?'

'I mean, Reds, this band is we band. This is the Calvary Hill people band; man, we ain't want to be no Gay Calvary Hill or anything like that just to get a few free jerseys and some fresh paint on the pans.'

'Nobody can't take away the band, man,' Reds said.

Reds couldn't see. To him it was just like the project work, the Crash Programme. We support them, they support we.

'You see Desperadoes? You see Tokyo? You see Sun Valley?'

'I ain't see no difference. Is just that they looking newer and they playing in concerts and the fellars from the band getting work. That is all I see.'

'You-all better don't get no sponsors in the band.'

'Take it easy, Premier,' Reds said.

When he heard that Terry and Reds was having talks with Fuller Brothers, he went to Terry.

'Terry, we can't have no sponsors in this band,' he said.

'Can't?'

'Can't!'

'Can't? You making joke, man.'

'You going to kill me, then?'

'Kill you?'

'Yes, kill me. 'Cause that is what you will have to do to bring a sponsor in this band.'

Never one to say much, Terry grunted, then smiled. But, Fisheye had his own plan, and that year he put it into operation. He began to fight again. Sponsors did not like violence in bands. Indeed, one of the conditions of sponsorship was no misbehaving in the band.

That Carnival he cuffed down a fellar from Highlanders, a new band from Laventille, and on the Tuesday of the same Carnival, he had people scampering from Park Street when he began throwing bottles at Dixie Land. And then he got in a fight with some members of his own band who were trying to restrain him. The following year it was the same thing. Bands had to leave Port of Spain early and go home because of him. It began to look, the newspapers reported, that hooliganism was coming back into Carnival again. But Fisheye didn't mind it. He didn't hear any more talk about Fuller Brothers. And then, last year the band threatened to put him out if he didn't behave. 'I'll behave,' he said, and as soon as they reached down Frederick Street he hit a man from San Juan All Stars with the end of the flag, and when the fellar started to argue he moved in to fight. The police arrested him that year. Fellars started to whisper that they didn't want him in the band. Daphne pleaded with him. He tried to explain, but she didn't understand, and so he had to let her taste his hand. Suddenly he was a warrior again, and in the midst of the peace, the decency of the steelbands, the well-behaved emasculated warriors, Calvary Hill, because of Fisheye, had a bad name. And here and there odd fellars from other bands began to have fights. He hoped that it would catch on. He wished warriorhood would come back again to the steelbands. He alone couldn't carry the full brunt of the fighting that was needed to change things, not against all the bands, not with members of his own band against him. And even though he had some young fellars with him, fellars who had come strong from the country or off the city streets, with broad shoulders and long empty hands, as he himself had come, feeling the weight of their uselessness, wishing for something to do, something to hold up, a banner, not caring what the cause was, looking for a fight, something to give them a name, a place – for the steelbands didn't give fellars that again – these fellars just wasn't enough; he really wanted an army of warriors to take back the bands, to take back the streets and alleys, the hills and the lanes from the Fuller Brothers and Sampoco Oil, and Cicada Cigarettes. But, fellars didn't understand.

And now, tonight, with Carnival two weeks off, Reds had just come to tell him that the fellars in the committee wanted to speak to him.

'Me? What they want to see me for?' he had asked, sitting on the culvert in front his house, where Aldrick would find him later.

'They . . . we don't want no fighting in the band. This year we want a clean Carnival.'

'For the sponsors?'

Reds' voice had an edge to it, and he didn't have that stupid smartman, triumphant giggle in his voice. 'Fisheye, times change. Times change, man. This ain't long time. We ain't bad Johns again. Everybody getting sponsors.'

'What we is now, Reds? What we is?'

'The fellars serious. They want to suspend you, if you can't behave. I tell them I'll come and talk to you.'

'Suspend me! Suspend me? They want to suspend me from Calvary Hill band. Because of your fucking sponsors, you want to suspend Fisheye? Reds, all of us is man; but, you-all going to have to kill me. If you try to put me out this band, I going to mash up every pan.'

'Don't say that, man,' Reds said softly, his voice tightening, toughening. 'Don't say that. The fellars wouldn't like to hear that. Don't say that, man.'

'What else I could say. Tell them I waiting here. They know where I stand.'

And he was sitting there on the culvert in front his house, his cutlass resting on the ground and out of sight, all kinda evil popping into his head, listening to the band practising up the Hill, wondering where he could get a sledge-hammer from for, really, if they put him out the band he was going to mash up every drum in the steelband. So when he heard the call, he tensed himself, his foot feeling for the cutlass to make sure it was where he wanted it, for he thought it was one of the fellars from the band; but when he looked he saw it was Aldrick, the dragon man, and his little stepson.

'Aye, Fish, what happening?' Aldrick's tone was friendly, almost cheerful now. On his walk with the boy, his anger had cooled, and he had found himself wondering what the hell he was sticking his nose into Fisheye business for. What could he really tell Fisheye? Fisheye had charge of the boy, and if he wanted to beat him, what could he (Aldrick) do?

'Shoulda go and lift some weights before I come and talk to him,' Aldrick thought. 'And learn some jujitsu.' And it was in this spirit that he approached Fisheye.

'What the hell you doing there alone on the culvert, man?'

Fisheye didn't answer, and Aldrick might have suspected that all was not right; for this manner of approach, this aggressive and anticipatory and conciliatory humour was the means by which men said to each other what they had to say, while avoiding conflict. 'I just bringing home your little son. I hear you does beat him for nothing.'

'So what?'

'So,' he plunged on, for he was aware of the boy standing tensely beside him. 'So, I come to warn you: If you beat him again I going straight to the gym and lift some weights and learn some jujitsu and come back for you.'

'I ain't making joke tonight,' Fisheye said coldly.

'If you think is joke I making, touch him,' Aldrick said, maintaining his tone.

'I ain't making joke tonight,' Fisheye said. 'That's what's wrong with this Hill: we have too much people making joke. What it is you come to tell me?'

'What I come to tell you?' Aldrick repeated the question, his voice changing at his hurt to a humble falsetto, confused by his shame now that Fisheye had refused to play the game. And it wasn't that he was afraid of Fisheye. He had learnt time and time again that it was useless to fear a man. If you did get into a fight, what you had to do was make sure that you put in a few good blows, so that the man, even if he was stronger, even if he beat you, would know that he was in a battle too. And as he stood there framing his answer in his shame, he heard Fisheye addressing the boy, his voice, soft and firm and a little tired: 'You, go inside. You coming home after dark and telling people how I beating you. Go inside. Later, I will deal with you.'

'What I come to tell you?' Aldrick repeated, his tone changed, accusing Fisheye of not playing the game. 'Nothing. I just bring your boy home. He was helping me with my dragon costume.' And he had turned then, very soberly, very chastened, and began to walk away, so that Fisheye, in spite of his own condition, impressed by Aldrick's dignity, decided to explain why he was not tonight playing the game, said:

' You hear what happening?'

'I ain't hear nothing,' Aldrick said in his new voice.

' You ain't hear they putting me out the band?'

' You . . . ? Out the band?'

'Their sponsors. They want musicians. They don't want men again.'

'Well . . .'

Perhaps the very confusion of Aldrick's 'well', the very uncertainty and resignation it breathed, angered Fisheye anew, so that he got up from where he was sitting:

'Well, tell them for me, they better look out. They know me. I could dead any time. Tell them . . .'

'Tell them?' Aldrick asked softly. 'Tell them? You know me, man; I ain't no messenger.'

'I ain't know who one damn soul is on this Hill. I thought we had men, but now I don't know who nobody is.'

'I still have to talk to you about the boy,' Aldrick said, turning to leave.

' You better don't talk that talk tonight.'

'When I lift the weights I will talk,' Aldrick said.

'Lift plenty,' Fisheye said.

Aldrick walked home very slowly. He was not happy

with himself at all. He had no right to get involved in the first place. Why did he get himself involved at all?

Maybe you getting soft in truth, he thought, as he entered the Yard.

His mind ran to Sylvia. He didn't want to think of her. He was already thinking too much about her.

'You's a dragon, man,' he thought. 'A dragon can't t'ink 'bout these things.'

'Hey, Aldrick!'

The voice startled him, but he immediately saw the teeth in the shyly smiling face on the steps. It was the Indian fellar, Parry or Singh or something – he never could remember his name.

'Okay!' Aldrick said, continuing to walk, for, although the fellar lived in the Yard Aldrick did not consider him a friend.

'You taking a stroll?'

Aldrick was about to walk on, but he felt tugged by the effort in the voice at friendliness, and he slowed down.

'Yea. How it going with you?' Aldrick said, without great vigour.

'I just cooling out. You want a cigarette?'

The Indian fellar had risen and had drawn from his breast pocket a new pack of Anchor, and stepped forward with it. Aldrick was thinking to refuse.

'I have a whole pack,' the fellar said.

'Okay.'

The fellar handed him the pack and produced a match. 'You could take a few, if you want, you know. I have a whole pack.'

Aldrick took out one cigarette and held it to the flame that the Indian produced. He felt awkward. It was the first time he was speaking to this fellar. He didn't know what to say.

'Thank you,' Aldrick said, making to move on.

'How your dragon costume coming along?' the Indian asked a bit nervously.

'Okay. It coming on okay.' Aldrick wished he had some-thing more to say, that they had something more in common. But he really didn't know this man. 'It kinda quiet tonight, eh!'

'I sit down here listening to the steelband,' the Indian said.

' Yes. With Carnival coming, they practise 'til late . . . Well, I goin' in.'

'All right. You could take a few cigarette if you want, you know. I have a whole pack.'

'Is okay,' Aldrick said, moving off.

'I name Pariag,' the Indian said. 'I living right there. I does see you all the time, but, we never talk.'

'No. We never talk,' Aldrick said.

'I is a A-one all fours player, you know.'

'A-one?'

'I from New Lands, and it ain't have a better all fours player there than me and Seenath. You does play all fours?'

'A little,' Aldrick said. 'Well, I goin' in now.'

'I see you-all playing a game on Sunday morning by the shoemaker.'

'Those fellars could play, you know,' Aldrick said, beginning to move on.

'If Seenath was down here I would have a partner, and then I coulda go and play. Who's your partner?'

'Philo. You know him? The calypsonian. Thin, smiling fellar?'

'If I had a partner and all-you give me an invite I would play.'

'But everybody have their partner, and I don't know anybody, so . . .'

Aldrick was moving slowly towards his own abode. He didn't know what to say. He had been taken by surprise.

'I hope you ain't feel funny as I talk so much,' Pariag said.

'Well . . . no,' Aldrick said, giving his words a kind of finality as a signal of his leave-taking, moving on now, but in truth, he found it a little strange that after maybe two years living in the Yard, Pariag had chosen this night to speak to him. And it was only afterwards, when he was inside and lying on his bed, thinking of the day's events, the boy, Basil, Fisheye, and Sylvia crowding his brain, that his mind ran on Pariag, and he thought: 'Shit! I never try to talk to him in the two years either.'

The Spectator

This Hill is home for thousands. They leave the country estates – Manzanilla, Sangre Grande, Cocal, Cedros – where they work the cocoa and coconuts for next to nothing for too long, and come to town to stay at a cousin or uncle or aunt or friend until they get their own place. They come with country all over their face, their shoulders broad from cutlassing cocoa and felling mora trees, with caps on, cheap silver chains around their necks, their socks peeping out bold below the fold of their trousers, walking in a kind of slow, rolling crawl, trying to look like town-men; and a few months later, cap gone, slim, cool, matchstick in mouth, they coasting in the swing of the city, asking a man for a cigarette, shouting full-lunged to a friend across the street, moving up Calvary Hill as if they own it.

Not so with Pariag. After two years he was still a stranger on this Hill, and even fellars he had watched come in long after him were looking at him as if it was he who was the new one. This more than anything about the Hill burnt Pariag, for the main reason he had come to the city to live was so that he could join up with people, be part of something bigger than just New Lands sugar estate, be more than just a little country Indian, cutting sugarcane in the day, cutting grass for the cattle in the evening, and, on Sundays, playing all fours in front the playground with Seenath, Bali and Ramjohn.

Ever since he was a small boy he had wanted to break out of the little village world where he had watched his brothers and his father and grandfather work, bound still in that virile embrace to the sugarcane estate to which his grandfather had been the first to be indentured, renewing their indenture year after year as if it were an inheritance that no repeal of law could force them to relinquish, unwilling to step beyond the boundaries of the village, remaining to get hooked into the world of Ramlochan, his father's eldest brother who by some miracle of work and luck and cunning had become the fastest growing businessman in New Lands, employing one by one his relatives, not only giving them work and paying them money, but having a say in who should marry who, who should buy what property, and who at times the others should refuse to talk to, living a kind of governorship of the clan, requiring them to be always indebted to him for some loan of money or some more subtle favour, as if it was only in a relationship of constant dependence they could express for him that love he felt they ought to owe him.

It seemed to Pariag that he had been too long in all this: too long in the village, too long in the sugarcane, too long meek and silent before his uncle, and while he had nothing against his success, indeed, was proud of it – for wasn't his grandfather, shrivelled up and thin and bent now like a piece of copper wire, his days spent sunning himself bare-backed in the front yard, not witness to where they had come from – he longed to go beyond the cows and grass and cane, out beyond the droning chant of the pundit, into a world where people could see him, and he could be some-body in their eyes; for this Trinidad was itself a new land, and he had not seen it yet, nor had it seen him. So he had decided, and nothing his father said could change his mind. He was going to leave the village.

'This young generation!' his father wailed. 'This young generation. Your uncle wouldn't like this, you know.'

'Kill me, Boya!' his mother cried, thin and plaintive. 'Send your own mother to her grave.'

But he knew that his mother liked to dramatize and exaggerate.

'The boy want to married,' his uncle said. 'I know a man in Tabaquite with a daughter just to age.'

'I ain't ready to get married yet,' he told his father, after the arrangements had been made for him to go and visit the girl. 'And besides, I want to choose a girl for myself. I is the one going to have to live with she.'

'For yourself?' his father asked. 'For yourself? You think you getting married for yourself? You think I get married for myself? You hear how you talking already and you ain't even leave this house yet.'

'But I never even see the girl, Pa.'

'You will see her. Your other uncle will carry you.'

So he went to see the girl, with the hope that he would find some fault with her and would therefore be able to say no.

She was a tall girl, half a head taller than he, and slim like a rice stalk, with hair down to her waist, and when she smiled her front teeth jutted out beneath her upper lip. She lived in a big old ramshackle wooden house with the country smell of green grass and dried cow dung about it; and as she sat there an arm's length away from him, her five sisters, all very thin and with the same jutting teeth when they smiled, came out and peeped at him and giggled. The father, a smiling man with baggy pants and a matchstick to pick his teeth, looked like he liked to talk a lot. He sat down with this wide smile on his face, and, in his eyes, a look of glee, as if he had already struck a master bargain. Looking at this man, Pariag saw himself, middle-aged, with two cows and nine children and the sugarcane field around him. He wanted to bolt. He wanted to run; but the girl was looking at him.

'What you name?' he asked her, kinda tough.

'Dolly,' she said. She was trembling.

'I is Boya. You ever . . . you ever went to Port of Spain?' as if he himself was familiar with the city.

She shook her head a little sadly, as if apologizing for being so country, so ignorant, and also with disappointment at not being able to please him. And then he saw in her eyes that she believed in him, believed that he was more than country, that he had dreams.

' You going to have to live in Port of Spain,' he said.

So he married the girl and left New Lands and found this place on Calvary Hill. It was one big room downstairs in a building where four families lived. He and Dolly were the only Indians in the Yard. He slung his hammock across the room, and they moved in.

The first job he got was with Seepersad, an Indian businessman from Tunapuna. The job was to go around with another fellar, on a van driven by Seepersad's third son, Vishnu, buying empty bottles which were to be washed and later re-sold to rum companies and drugstores at what must have been a good profit. The work wasn't too hard; and at first, Pariag really looked forward to going out on the van, riding all over the city and its outskirts, getting to know places like Belmont and St James, Woodbrook and Laventille and St Ann's. Some nights he would slip away from Dolly and go to Royal Theatre and see cowboy movies, and in the day, riding the van, the wind blowing through his hair, he imagined himself a cowboy riding the range.

The van picked him up at half past five every morning, and he worked right through till nightfall. The best thing in the job was bargaining with the people from whom they bought the bottles. He really liked to bargain, not so much to reduce the price they asked as much as to enter into conversation with them, to get to know them and to let them see that he was more than just a little country Indian out of New Lands.

'This boy, this thin one here, with the crooked nose and the hair plastered down on his head, could argue and beat down price, eh,' they said. 'Aye! What you name?'

'Boya,' he said.

He liked it when they asked his name; and it really was nice when afterwards, going back in to an area that they had touched before, people would come out and call him by name: 'Aye! Boya, I have six bottles here and I want three cents apiece for them.' And he would sigh and pass a hand across the side of his hair and look important and go to Vishnu, Seepersad son, and say: 'Vishnu, give this lady there three cents.'

'Three cents? You crazy or what, boy. This ain't the Salvation Army. This is business. Three cents!' And Vishnu would pay a penny.

Except for one or two cases, however, people didn't know his name. To them he was Bottles. Everybody working on the van was Bottles. And when people came out with their few bottles, they would say, 'Bottles, how much you giving me for these nine bottles I have here. The next van give a penny and a half, how much you giving? A penny?'

'That's the price, lady. I can't help the price.'

After three months, Pariag grew tired of the job. It had become boring, and he really wasn't getting to know anybody, and people weren't getting to know him, weren't interested in knowing him. More and more he was simply Bottles. Seepersad had started him off at five dollars a week, working seven days, half-day Saturdays, and had offered a commission on every hundred bottles the van brought in, to be split three ways – between he, Pariag, and Vishnu, and the other boy, Balliram, who stood in the van whole day shouting: 'Boddles! Empty Boddles! Buying empty boddles!' singing it like a song whole day, trying to sound like Kamaludin Mohammed on the Indian programme over the radio. Balliram's ambition was to be an announcer for one of the movie houses promoting East Indian pictures; and whenever the van was passing through a place where there were no houses he would practise his announcing: 'Tha Princess Cenemar proudly presents-ah for your-ah weekend-ah entertainment-ah, tha wonderful-ah, tha marvellous-ah, tha magnificent, tha colossal-ah motion picture. Winnah of five academy awards-ah: Choti Baheen-ah, starring tha masterful Dilip Kumar and the exciting-ah Ramjanee Roy with-ah dances by Helen-ah.' Balliram was really serious about his announcing. Sometimes when he was talking ordinary, he would slip in a little announcing practice: 'Bring-ah that boddle-ah here, ma lady-ah,' so he really didn't care too much about the commission. He was getting his announcing practice; so when Pariag asked him if he was getting his share of the commission, Balliram said: 'Commission! Boy, don't ask those kinda question round here. The last boy here ask that kinda question one day, the next day he wasn't here. They don't like those question here at all.'

The bottles business began driving Pariag crazy, and nobody was telling him anything about the commission, and he was afraid to ask. He began to dream about bottles – bottles floating down on the sea, bottles piled up from street to sky. One night he dreamed a whole pile of bottles was raining out of the sky upon him, all size bottles: pints, quarts, half gallon, gallon. That was when he decided to leave the job. But he was thinking about his commission. He kinda hinted it to Vishnu, but Vishnu kept on combing his hair and searching his face for buttons to burst between his fingernails. From that day Pariag began systematically and accidentally to break one or two bottles as soon as he got the chance. That whole month he broke bottles until he satisfied himself that their cost covered his part of the commission. Then, one morning he got up and told Dolly that he wasn't going to work. The van came at half past five as usual, and Seepersad son remained out in the street blowing his horn; blowing his horn; and he just remained in his hammock and listened to the horn blow. He wished somebody would go outside and give Seepersad son a good cuff in the mouth for disturbing people at half past five in the morning. He didn't like Vishnu, with his hair combed up high in front his head,

like Tony Curtis, and a handkerchief in his back pocket.
Every time the van stopped Vishnu tilted down the rear
view mirror to comb his hair and squeeze a pimple out his
face.

He had worked for Seepersad for four months and he
hadn't made a friend. Balliram, the other boy who worked
on the truck was Indian too, but Balliram used to try to
push him around because he knew he was from the
country. Balliram was from San Juan. He liked to cuss and
get on like Creole people. He was always boasting about
his Creole girl friends and about the dances he went to.
The biggest thing in his life was talking to Pariag about the
time he played masquerade portraying Viva Zapata in
Corregidors steelband. Balliram was a fool. Shouting
boddles on the van whole day was exactly what suited him.

After Pariag left that job, he took the little money that he
had saved and bought a basket and a big iron pot and some
peanuts and channa, a tasty bean that was a favourite of the
town people. He started selling roasted peanuts and boiled
and fried channa. On Sundays and weekends he sold at the
Savannah at the football games; on Saturdays he went to the
race track in the season.

People in the Yard were now seeing more of him,
because he came straight home after the football games. In
fact, he walked home with the spectators who lived up
Calvary Hill. It was kinda nice walking home with them,
and in a secret kinda way he felt himself part of the crowd,
part of the people, part of town; but, in truth, all he would
do would be to listen to them argue. They could really
argue. And he listened to them argue about the players and
the teams they supported – the popular teams: Malvern,
Maple, Colts.

Colts was his team from since he was a boy in New
Lands, long before he even saw them play. That time it was
the Colts of the Harding Brothers – Bertie and Jim – and
Dudley Husbands and Horace Lovelace, Pepperwine they
called him, after a racehorse of that name, and he used to sit

home in New Lands, reading the newspapers and see Pepperwine racing down the left wing, bringing the crowd to its feet, sending the ball crashing across the goal mouth. Colts was still his team, but they thought he didn't know anything about football. They just figured that because he was a country Indian football was foreign to him. One day he was bold. Three fellars were discussing the upcoming Colts–Maple game. They looked like all-right fellars, and he felt that he could talk to them. 'I like Colts,' he said, and they all stopped walking and looked at him. Then the Maple supporter said, 'Haii! What the hell this Indian know about football? You ever see a Indian on a football team?' Pariag felt very chilly. He didn't say nothing. He slowed down and let them walk ahead of him. After that he never liked Maple. He had no sympathy with them even when they were playing Casuals, the local white team.

Though he kept to himself now, Colts remained his team. He was always thinking to shout, 'Colts!' dying to shout, 'Colts!' so that people would see him, identify him as belonging somewhere, talk with him, let him be one of them, surround him and engage him the way they did with the man who sold snowball in a pushcart at football games in the Savannah.

Everybody knew him as 'Colts'. Generations of people knew him as a staunch supporter of Colts Football team, relinquishing whatever name he had received at baptism to bear his team's name; and oh, was to see all the schoolboys rushing to buy snowball from him, shouting 'Colts! Colts! Colts!' as if they were eager to recognize and accept him, and, by some kind of magical rebounding, be themselves recognized and accepted. He had a word he used to say. He used to say, 'Right, man! Right, man!' as an acknowledgement and salutation, with that ease and generosity, as if he knew that he would forever belong here to the earth and to the Savannah and to the fans and the children. 'Right, man!' And he would ask if you wanted your snowball with condensed milk on top it, or if you wanted green syrup or red syrup or brown. He had a brown syrup that was guava flavoured. That was nice. That was real nice. Some people used to ask for all three, and he used to dip the shaved ice skilfully into the different pans of syrup, dip! dip! dip! flick it up so as not to let the syrup leak from the juicy snowball, hand it over with one hand, and receive payment with the other.

'Don't rush me!' he used to say sometimes; pleasantly, as an admonition to hurry people who wanted to come the same minute and get served right away, but more as if talking to himself, as if saying to himself, Be cool! Be cool! *'Don't rush me'* – when the crowd around his cart was thick at half time, and everybody wanted to get his snowball in a hurry to rush back and get a seat before the second half of the game began. *'Don't rush me!'*

And sometimes out of sheer exuberance, out of a sweet admiration at himself, a kind of amazement at his own speed and agility in dispatching so many snowballs – shaving the ice and cupping it and dipping it into at least two pans of syrup and maybe pouring condensed milk atop it, out of this sweet sense of wonder and of acceptance of the magical clean swiftness and nervelessness of his actions, he would shout as if to steady himself: 'Colts! Colts!' As if to steady himself and salute himself, as if to say, Lord, look how I quick! Look at my speed! 'Colts!' And some of the people around, sharing in the marvelling and the admiration, warming to his salute and wanting to join in it, would chorus, 'Colts! Colts!' and he, Colts, would say it again, accepting their recognition and salute, 'Colts!' So that there grew in the Savannah on an evening a song chorused and chanted for Colts, a song to the man and the football team and the Savannah and the fans and the world.

Pariag wished he could become part of this, this living, and his eyes misted as he watched Colts, a short, thin, greying man with a cap on, in the midst of people, being himself, earning a living, and belonging. For Colts belonged to everybody, to every team, all of them, even the supporters of the fiercest rivals of Colts, all of them would seek out Colts to buy snowball from and to say a word to, in their very bantering and rivalling, upkeeping him, keeping up in him that sense of support and belonging to something which, on his own, he had made his own; and no one arguing with him ever dreamt that any logic or anger or something more mysterious could make him change his allegiance.

'Colts, we going to whip you today! Colts, is going to be hard today. Five! Five goals we scoring on you today!' – rivals would tease, and Colts would say, 'Neverhappen!' That is another word he used to say, 'Neverhappen!'

But now and again, stung by a remark from a rival supporter, he would begin to stammer and want to argue, and somebody around his cart, someone who knew him and who recognized that he, Colts, was an essence, beyond the rivalry of the men on the field, beyond even football itself, would shout a warning: 'Colts!' a sharp ringing cry to force him back to himself, to bring him back to the reality of his essence and symbolhood; and recognizing this, Colts would immediately cool down and start a joke with the very man with whom he had wanted to argue a while before. 'All right! All right!' he would say, and he would smile that littleboy-oldman smile that creased his face and showed his teeth, and shake his head as if he had caught himself slipping by allowing himself to be teased, and with this wisdom that even he was vulnerable, he would slap his leg, and before the shout, half-mocking, warm and exuberant, could leave his throat, those spectators who had seen it all, who knew him, would be already joining in to make the chorus, 'Colts!' forgiving and upholding him, even as he made his own appeasing cry.

Pariag liked to sell his channa and peanuts next to Colts' cart.

'Hey, Indian, how it going today?' Colts would ask, and he would answer, 'Okay.'

Sometimes, caught behind the playing field, out of sight of the game, Colts would stammer out, at the sound of an uproar from the crowd, 'Wh-who score?' And Pariag, who always kept track of these things in his very quiet way, would tell him. Their conversation did not go far beyond this. They just had the common courtesies between two people selling; that was all. And really he didn't expect too much more. In the Savannah with the excitement of football games, it was hard to make friends. To people there he was Channa Boy. That was his new name.

Okay! In the Savannah and on the streets he was Channa Boy. People only saw the basket of channa and peanuts in his hand, but, in the Yard on Alice Street, it was different. They saw him come in the Yard and go out. They saw him open a door and go in. He was living there. They saw his wife fetching water at the pipe, scrubbing over the tub, hanging clothes on the line to dry. They had to know that he was somebody, a person.

On Sunday morning they had an all fours game down the street, in front Mr Alphonso shoemaker shop. He passed in front the place many times and stopped to look at them – Aldrick, Philo, a fellow named Popie and, sometimes, Mr Guy – but they never invited him in. For Carnival he had seen the whole Yard wild, everybody getting set to play masquerade, everybody looking to buy costume, people going to calypso tent to hear calypsonians sing, people going to listen to the steelband practise. They never one day, not one of them say, 'Boya', or 'Channa Boy' as some of them in the Yard called him, they never said, 'Channa Boy, come and go,' or, 'We going so and so place, come with us.'

In truth, he didn't know much about Carnival. He had never played masquerade, and he had never beaten a steel pan. In New Lands Carnival was just a few wild Indians and maybe a robber or two and a few stickfighters playing under Bholai shop. Only the stickfight battles held any interest for him, and one day, carried away by the drums, he had jumped into the stickfight ring, but Seenath had pulled him out. Real Carnival was a city thing, a Creole thing. Nobody in the country had all that money to throw away on a costume; though, and this was his secret that he had never told anybody: he had often thought that when he came to Port of Spain he would play masquerade in a Big Nose sailor band, with his tin of face powder and streams of confetti to throw on all the pretty girls he passed in the streets, or of playing Ali Baba in a band, with a curved sword and a big fat turban, like a genie, and taking out a photograph of himself and sending it back to New Lands for his family and Bali and Seenath and Ramjohn to see.

Maybe he should have approached them. Maybe he should have gone to one of them and said, 'Listen, I is a card player from New Lands. I want a hand in your all fours game,' and, when they questioned him, tell them about the games he used to play – he and Seenath against Jhogi and a Creole fellar named Titus. He didn't know about steelband and Carnival, but he coulda told them about all fours. But, no. He felt that he was the stranger, and that it was in their place to invite him out. He was shy too, and he didn't want to push up himself to anybody to be insulted or laughed at. But, after two years on Calvary Hill, no one had made any effort to be friends with him; instead, he could sense them watching him, watching him as if they couldn't trust him, as if they shared among themselves a secret which they were afraid he would discover, and were debating whether to reveal it to him or to chase him out of their midst entirely. He made one friend though.

They called him Fisheye. He was a tall, black fellar with eyes bulging out his head, and he stood at the corner of the street, a guardian of the gate to the Hill; and one day, he said to him:

'Hey, Indian!'

So he went over.

'You living up here?'

'Yes. Is up here I living.'

'Where?'

'Alice Street.'

Fisheye had looked him over as if deciding what to do with him.

' You look like a okay fellar. Gimme a shilling.'

Pariag did not hesitate. He took out the coin almost gladly and gave it over, and so began between himself and this Fisheye a relationship in which every time they met, Fisheye asked him for a shilling which he felt compelled to give. He didn't like the arrangement, but in some strange kind öf way he felt that it joined him more firmly to the Hill.

' You don't see that you is Indian and they is Creole,' Dolly said to him, when he told her about it.

'No, Dolly. No. It ain't that. They don't know me. They don't know the kinda man I is.' And he believed that.

When Christmas came the Yard prepared to celebrate, not as big as Carnival but a man bought a couple bottles of rum and put them down in his house to offer his friends when they came by, the children in the Yard had balloons and the women put up new curtains. Miss Cleothilda put up new curtains and polished her chairs and varnished some things and boiled a ham and she baked a cake before Christmas Day and sent a piece wrapped in fancy paper to everybody in the Yard, and she sent a piece for Dolly.

' You see, Dolly. You see. They is people,' Pariag told her, when she showed him the cake that Miss Cleothilda had sent, for it really looked to him that at last the Yard was ready to admit them as friends.

'They is people, girl. And we is people to them, even though they is Creole and we is Indian.' It warmed him so much, the gift of cake, that he took his money and bought two bottles of rum to have in the house in case the neighbours dropped in.

Christmas morning wasn't bright, but a few fellars from the neighbourhood passed around, going from house to house on Alice Street, singing and making merry. They didn't have no first class instruments: Philo had a guitar, Aldrick had a toy flute, Popie had a mouth organ and the rest of them had bottles and spoons, but it didn't matter, the music was nice. It was Christmas. Five of them, two of them barebacked, and all of them sweet with liquor, going from house to house, singing and playing music on their instruments. They went upstairs by Mr Guy and Miss Cleothilda, and Pariag could hear them laughing and talking and saying, 'Merry Christmas!' and Miss Cleothilda fussing around in her show-off way, telling them, 'Look ham! Eat ham! Look cake! Eat cake! Everything is yours. I make this for you.'

Afterwards they came downstairs and went by Miss Olive who, with seven children and little money coming in, couldn't have had any big preparation, but they remained at her place, singing and laughing and making jokes, and blowing up the children's balloons; and, Pariag got nervous and excited because he was sure that after they left Miss Olive they would come next at him, so he opened the door, and Dolly washed the five glasses they had, and he took out a bottle of the rum and put it on the table on which Dolly had spread their tablecloth that they had never used, since they had never had visitors, and he chipped up a piece of ice and put it in a bowl, and he had a bottle of pepsi-cola and a bottle of ginger ale and a bottle of plain water, and Dolly had made some roti, and she put them on the table, with some curried mango in a bowl, and a bottle of hot pepper sauce that she had got from her mother, and they waited. The band left Miss Olive and it went over to Aldrick's room, and then it went over the fence to where Miss Caroline was living, and Pariag was sure that they were leaving him for last because he was new. He waited there, he and Dolly, he, with a pressed shirt on, and she with her hair combed down and tied in plaits. They waited, with the ice melting in the bowl, and the roti and the curried mango getting cold. The band never came. They never came. Pariag just didn't hear the music any more, and when he looked outside, they had left Miss Caroline's house.

'They don't want your friendship, Boya,' Dolly told him. 'They go by everybody and they leave you out. You don't see?'

'*I* shoulda invite them in. This is my place. *I* shoulda go to the door and call them and say, "Neighbour, come in. Come and take a drink with me for Christmas. I is a Indian from New Lands and I ain't have no prejudice. We is all people. Come in!" How they could know I make preparation for them if I didn't tell them? How they will know that if they come in here they wouldn't embarrass me because I ain't have a drink to offer them? They don't know.'

'And they don't care either,' Dolly said.

'They don't know me,' Pariag insisted. 'They don't know the kinda man I really is.'

He thought about this incident for the whole day, and he didn't even open the rum.

'You know what it is, Dolly,' he said to her when they were in bed.

'What what is, Boya?' She was tired from the tension of the waiting, and from sharing the unhappiness that Pariag felt; and she was afraid of this place. It was all in her voice.

'They not *seeing* me, that is what it is. That is it; they don't *see* me. You see?'

'How they could not see you?'

'Well, I ain't big. I mean, I ain't have no huge muscles, and I don't sound tough, and I ain't tough, and I can't fight, and don't know how to play steelband or sing calypso, and I don't know much about Carnival. . . . You see?'

'No. They don't see you,' she said, testingly, still waiting to understand.

He had always wondered about Balliram, the boy who had worked on the bottles van with him. Balliram liked to pretend he was a Creole. He understood better now. But he, Pariag, was not a Creole, and he didn't intend to play one. But he wanted them to see him.

'If maybe I had a car, Dolly . . .'

'A car, Boya? Where we will park it?'

'A bicycle, then.' And immediately he knew that that was it. 'A green bike with a carrier. We could sell channa and peanuts and barra and doubles. And put a sign on it. And a bell, a big bell to ring. They must see me when I riding down the street. Eh? Eh?'

Dolly was silent for a while. Then she smiled, catching his excitement. The bicycle appealed to her. It was a good idea. Without cows here in this place and grass to cut the days took too long. Barra and doubles would make good business, better business than channa and peanuts. She would make the delicacies herself, and Pariag would sell them on his bicycle.

'We could buy it, yes,' she said.

The idea seized them. To Pariag, getting that green carrier bicycle was his fixed star, and he began to save to buy it, cash, because he didn't know too much about credit in this city. And all the little slights, all the hard little stings, he felt he could bear now, for he knew that the day would come when everybody, on Alice Street, on Calvary Hill, maybe even people of Port of Spain, would see him.

After one year, that day was three days away, and he felt so excited that he even got bold and made himself known to Aldrick, the fellar in the Yard who was the king dragon in Carnival.

And now on the Saturday afternoon one week before Carnival, Pariag was finally on his bicycle, riding up Henry Street, going from Port of Spain to his home on Alice Street.

With Carnival just one week away, the city was hot confusion: people moving in crazy streams up sidewalks, across the open streets, their laughter ringing above the music of the rush traffic and the steelband rhythms and calypso tunes blasting from juke boxes and record shops, their mingled scents rising as a special incense in the steaming heat. For once, Pariag felt bigger than Port of Spain, watching the people from his bicycle, the fellars with beers and rum in their hands, women with pieces of costume material, the tourists, white faces reddened with too much rum and sun, holding smiles of bewilderment as they swivelled their necks to gaze at the confusion into which they seemed pleased to have entangled themselves, about them an air of inquiry and surrender, as if they were searching for something, some part of themselves, which they had recently discovered that they had misplaced, that was to be found here, somewhere among these people, would turn up perhaps in one of those photographs which they so greedily took.

'Wheee!' Pariag thought as, crouched low over his bicycle, he bore his way through the maze of cars and trucks and carts, more hurry than anybody else to get home, making a swing away from a man who stepped out suddenly, carelessly, from behind a car to cross the street, grazing him, righting himself and sprinting off, looking back over his shoulder only when he was a safe distance away, to hear the fellow shout: 'Hey! Look at that crazy Indian! Look at him! Hey, like you don't want to live to see Carnival.'

'You see?' Pariag thought. 'You see? Already they start to see me.'

The Crazy Indian! He liked that name. The Crazy Indian; and he raised himself off his saddle, bent himself into a deeper crouch, the Crazy Indian racing up alongside cars, darting through the narrow spaces in the thick traffic, ringing his bell, listening to it sound its clear, wonderful triumphant announcement and warning. He liked it when people, hearing the bell, looked back and saw him coming, racing, bearing down upon them, dashed out his path. He liked it when they turned around and abused him. 'Haii! Look at that crazy fucking Indian! Look at him!' But his real pleasure lay ahead of him. Wait till the people in the Yard see him. Wait! He was so anxious to reach Alice Street.

His bicycle moved like oil; and in no time at all the Crazy Indian had reached the foot of Observatory Street. He was mad to ride his bicycle up against the One Way street, just for fun; but he got off and began to push it. He felt good. The city looked friendly now.

'I bet they invite me to play all fours now,' he thought. He could just see himself now – all fours at Mr Alphonso shoemaker shop on a Sunday morning, steelband practice, people calling calling out to him: 'Hello, Boya! Hello, Boya!' And he answering: 'Hello, Aldrick! Right-o, Philo!' 'You want to go and hear me sing in the tent tomorrow night, Boya?' And he answering: 'Not tomorrow. I tied up tomorrow; but Saturday. What about Saturday?' And for Christmas everybody coming in his house and singing and talking and making joke and having a good time, everybody, all the regular fellars, and he bringing out curried mango and roti; and when he walk down the street fellars stopping him: 'Come and take a drink with us before you go to work, man;' and he, saying: 'Later, man. Later.' Or may be if he was in the mood, saying: 'Okay, but one. Just one.'

Pariag was thrilled by his own vision, and he didn't even notice that he had reached the entrance to the Hill.

'Channa Boy!'

The words reached him like a slap, and his anger rose swiftly and stuck in his throat. He lifted his head slowly and turned to the voice, brushing aside a lock of hair that had fallen over his eyes.

Three fellars were leaning against the wall of the Chinee shop. One of them was Fisheye.

'Come!' Fisheye, holding his leaning pose, crooked a finger at him.

Come? Pariag thought. Come? He don't know is a big man he talking to. Come? But he guided his bicycle in

Fisheye's direction, smiling now, not the earlier smile of satisfaction and excitement, but a sickly effort to hide his rising anger.

'How you passing me so straight today, man?'

Fisheye's back was against the wall, one foot was on the ground, the sole of the other flat against the wall. A matchstick was at the corner of his mouth, and he was chewing it slowly, appreciatively, without separating his teeth.

'I . . . I didn't see you,' Pariag said, trying in his tone to establish a balance between proper respect and his own dignity. 'I . . . I really didn't see you.'

'You mean,' Fisheye said. He was perfectly still, eyes half closed, and chewing the matchstick gravely. 'You mean I so black you can't even see me in the day.' Then he opened his eyes and grinned, his lips curling off his teeth, his eyes shining, bulging. 'That will cost you two shilling, my friend.'

Pariag looked at him, hesitated. 'I don't know if I have two,' he said, maintaining that tone that gave Fisheye his respect, yet kept alive some idea of his own manness. He pushed his hand into his pocket, slowly, very conscious of his show of reluctance, wanting to make of it, the hesitation, a gesture of defiance. 'Things hard these days,' he said, feeling in his pocket, trying to identify the different coins by touch. Once he had brought out a dollar, and Fisheye had demanded it, and he had had to hand it over.

He came up with forty-two cents. He held the coins for a long moment, even while Fisheye's hand extended to receive them hung there. He let it hang for a few long seconds, then he smiled and dropped the coins into it.

'You have a new bike,' Fisheye said, pocketing the money and spitting out the chewed up matchstick.

'I have to try.'

'Just now you is a big shot, eh? Just now you going to start bouncing down people with your new bicycle, eh?'

'I wouldn't bounce you down, Fisheye,' Pariag said.

He turned away. He didn't bother to attempt to ride up the Hill. He pushed it. The beautiful exuberance had gone from him. But, there was one thing. He had called the man Fisheye to his face, for the first time.

'Straight to his face, I call him Fisheye,' Pariag said aloud. 'Straight to his face. Fisheye! Fisheye! Fisheye!'

Pariag was now atop the incline. The road sloped down for the rest of the way, then it flattened out into Alice Street. He mounted his Humber again; and now, in the saddle, the breeze beating against his face, chasing his hair, and sending his shirt ballooning, he coasted down the Hill, the bicycle tick-ticking, celebrating its newness, bringing to him again the beautiful sense of possession.

'Let him try and stop me when I going down a hill,' Pariag thought. 'I wouldn't bounce him down at all.'

He was the Crazy Indian again, weaving through potholes and garbage, making getaways from stray dogs. Then he reached the Yard. He would walk now.

Pariag was trembling, but as he approached the Yard he tried to think of himself as the Crazy Indian and to force a swagger into his gait. It was all for nothing. The only person in sight was one of Miss Olive's children, the boy Steve, a thin, raggedy child of six or seven. He had no pants on, and was swinging on the bottom half of the door to the room where he lived, trying to break it off. When he saw the bicycle he stopped in the middle of one of his swings and dragged a dirty palm across his nose, drawing from it a long, grey, elastic string of snot which he managed to plaster across one side of his face. He got down from the door, and, with a look of amazement and evil delight, began to move warily towards the new Humber which Pariag was now holding at standstill in the Yard

Pariag watched the boy come up to the bicycle, and already divining his intent, he said, 'Hey! Don't touch that!' But the boy was already caressing the back fender. For a moment he drew back, not really in response to Pariag's command, but savouring the feel of the smooth metal against his palm. His eyes moved over the bicycle, which had clearly hypnotized him now. It settled on the bell. And suddenly, eagerly, the boy grabbed the trigger of the bell and was ringing it. Before Pariag could move to dislodge him, the Yard filled with Miss Olive's other small children. Ragged clothes, dirty hands, they encircled Pariag and began to climb all over the bicycle.

'Haii! Move!' Pariag had to shout now, as he tried to chase them off; and above this his ears suddenly rang with a shattering scream: 'Miss Olive! Miss Olive! Come and see 'bout your children!' When he looked up it was to see Miss Cleothilda, her shoulders bare, a towel covering her brassiereless chest, leaning over her verandah, screaming at the top of her lungs as if somebody was being murdered. When he looked down he saw Miss Olive's huge frame in her doorway.

'Good . . . good afternoon,' Pariag said, trying to sound at ease.

'Mammy, a new bike! A new bike!' the children cried.

Pariag didn't realize that a woman of such size could move so swiftly. In one bound Miss Olive was out her door, had grabbed the first child and hurled him aside. Suddenly she was among the children, slapping and cuffing and heaving them away. It took less than one minute, this action. Miss Olive had scattered the children, pushed them inside and shut her door as if they had been exposed to some evil presence against which she must forever guard them. Pariag stood amazed.

'What is that going on down there?'

Mr Guy stood leaning over his verandah, a razor in one hand, and his face half covered with a shaving lather. Then Guy saw the bicycle.

'What? Who . . . ? Whose . . . ?' He didn't need to complete the question.

'He nearly kill the children for touching his bike,' Miss Cleothilda, her modesty still rescued by a bath towel, had

not recovered from whatever shock it was she had suffered.
'Nearly kill them.'

Pariag stood shocked before this accusation and con-
demnation. He looked around to see whether he had
brought anything else in with his bicycle, something
which would draw forth such severity from the Yard. He
shook his head. He didn't know. He stood there, looking at
the bicycle now, wondering what had he done, what law
had he broken. His mouth opened to ask, but Guy's face
disappeared, and as he turned to Miss Cleothilda, he saw
that the vigour of her indignation had caused the towel to
slide down and expose her breasts, and not wanting to add
impoliteness to whatever crime it was he had already
committed, he shifted his eyes from her, and just stood
there, hurt and confused and alone. He saw Dolly opening
the door to the room they lived in. He pushed the bicycle
towards her.

'What? What happen?' Dolly asked, seeing his face.

'I . . . I don't know,' Pariag said. 'I don't know,' and he
looked at the bicycle again.

6   A Call to the Dragon

In less than an hour the fact of Pariag's new bicycle had settled upon the Yard like a death. In that time Miss Cleothilda, who revelled in the drama of grief and misfortune, had closed her parlour and returned to her verandah where, costumed in green pedal pushers, a black scarf covering her head, and an old dress wound around her belly, she began to sing the hymn Rock of Ages in a thin, mournful voice which she punctuated with long silences, succeeding as she no doubt intended in presenting herself as weighed down by a bereavement about which she was too noble to complain. Mr Guy, shaven and sombre in his grey jacket and black polka-dot bow tie, came down the stairs, pressing a white handkerchief nervously against every spot of his ceaselessly perspiring face, and moved out of the Yard with an air of mission − an insulted, if not grievously injured party − as if he had decided to go directly to see his lawyer. Downstairs, Miss Olive eased open her front door to receive Miss Caroline, who slipped in heavy with that gossip and consolation found in those mourners who use the grief of their hostess as an excuse to enter and examine the quality and condition of her furniture and of the bed she slept on. Together, behind the closed door, in subdued tones filled with whispered exclamations of outrage, they engaged in a conversation which they interrupted nearly two hours later − the minute Miss Caroline spied Aldrick returning after an absence from the Yard since morning − to allow Miss Olive to dispatch her son Steve to inform Aldrick that, as the little boy put it, breaking into a wide grin of satisfaction the moment he had completed his rehearsed message: 'The Indian man buy a bike,' leaving Aldrick no wiser then, for in the instant of the boy's telling, Aldrick's mind was on other things: on the boy Basil, whom he had not seen since the night he took him home; on Sylvia, that child, woman, promise, challenge, whom he found himself daily watching, flitting about the Yard, her eyes, rising boldly to meet his, containing neither accusation nor invitation, kindling a kind of active uncaring, a kind of: 'Well if is so you want it is okay with me'; and it would be he, as the one more discomfited (oh, she was triumphant), vulnerable all of a sudden to the bite of an unfamiliar feeling of guilt that had begun pressing into him more firmly since the night he joked his way out of confronting Fisheye; it would be he who would feel the need to try with a smile to give the impression that he was in possession of some message of hope, some promise that she had a profit in; but it was a hope and a promise that as yet his mind had not imagined, and to discover it within himself he had begun to withdraw into himself. He had begun to feel the need to understand himself, to find out what things meant and why was he doing the things he was doing. It was a strange, uncomfortable thing with him, and it had quietened him down.

So that when Philo dropped in on him a day ago and said to him, in that bubbly way that he, Philo, had managed to maintain at age forty-two, as if he would forever be a boy captured by the amusing and breathless things of the world — he seemed to be alive in an immediate present, not yet considering the future and having dismissed the past — when Philo came that day, yesterday, and met him working on his dragon costume and said with delight: 'Yes! Yes, man! Your dragon good!' he wasn't surprised to hear himself say, 'Oh, fuck the dragon!'

'It's Sylvia, not so?' Philo said with that sympathetic grin, joined to him how men are joined together in their pursuit of a woman they all desire but against whom one, the one she chooses goes forth as hunter. 'Why you don't buy the costume for her?'

'Is not just a matter of a costume, man. Is her eyes: the way she does look at me.'

'Then, buy her the costume. Buy her the costume, then you could look in her eyes too.' Philo gave a suggestive laugh. 'If I had the money I would lend you just for it to happen.'

'T'ain't the costume alone. She's a woman with all those woman things in her, those woman wantings . . . I mean, she not asking for anything, but if you's her man, the world is what you will want to give her.'

'So you serious then?' Philo was alarmed. 'I thought . . . I thought she was just an adventure, a little side thing. Guy . . . I thought Guy was the serious one.'

'Guy? What Guy know 'bout woman?'

'What Guy . . . ? Guy could afford her, man.'

'Afford her costume.'

'Haii!' The exclamation jumped out of Philo, forced out of him almost in horror: 'You not serious about that girl, man? Eh?'

'Nah. I can't get serious about no woman; she just have me thinking, that's all. You know what I mean, man?

'You know, I use to say to myself: "Aldrick, you living the life. If it have one man in the world living the life is you – no wife, no child, no boss, no job. You could get up any hour of the day you want to, cuss who you want. Anywhere you go people like you. You is a favourite in the world. Anybody will give you a dollar just so. And for Carnival you's the best dragon in the whole fucking world" . . . and now this little stupid girl, this girl . . .'

'Have your head on,' Philo said, suddenly quite grave. 'I . . . I thought it was just the costume you wanted to give her.'

'T'ain't nutten, she just have me thinking, that's all.'

'Have your head on,' Philo said softly, as if he was more than a little afraid.

They had parted, with Philo talking in a thoughtful whisper, and looking at Aldrick as if from then on he would need to watch him much more carefully, as if he had discovered in him the potential for treason to a way of life they had shared so long, lived so long, that its very basis, its rationale had been forgotten and even he (Philo) to his fright could not, if he were called upon to do it immediately, defend it sensibly. 'Have your head on,' he said, a warning that now even he would need to heed.

So with his head so full, Aldrick really did not think of what the boy came hurriedly and said to him. And it wouldn't be until hours later, after deciding to go down town to Lucky Jordan to see if he could get a man to play him single-hand rummy, that he came outside to take a bathe, a towel around his shoulders, and his bathing trunks on, that he would encounter the changed mood of the Yard.

It was very quiet, and he might have explained it as that tiredness that fell on the Hill after most of the preparations for Carnival, that lull in which they rested themselves before they gathered themselves for the dancing and drinking and fucking and joking and masquerading of Carnival; but, as he reached the stand-pipe, he heard Miss Cleothilda singing Rock of Ages, her sighing punctuating it so mournfully that he looked up and saw her dragging herself across her verandah with no spirit at all, that the boy Steve came back before him, and he began to wonder whether in the boy's mumbling there was not some message to which the Yard's mood and Miss Cleothilda's performance were connected. And even as he strained to remember what words the boy might have uttered, Miss Cleothilda, abandoning her singing, and pretending not to see him, was summoning her last ounce of strength to call out to Miss Olive, a desperate plaintive cry that brought Miss Olive promptly into the Yard, so that she would be the one to recognize him, to say the single word: 'Aldrick!' welcoming him with a relief that suggested that he was the only one who could rescue her from the catastrophe which had overtaken them.

'Olive!' Miss Cleothilda sighed, 'you see what happening?' pitching her voice at Aldrick who had begun bathing at the pipe.

'Miss Cleothilda, I don't know . . . I don't know,' Olive said, fanning her face with her open palm.

'That is why I never trust them,' Miss Cleothilda was saying. 'They too sly and secretive. You could never know what going on with them. Turn, just turn your head, and they knife you in the back.'

'But how? How we coulda ever think to expect that from him?'

It was then, at these words from Miss Olive, that the boy's words re-formed in his mind: 'The Indian man buy a bike.'

'Twenty years I live here,' Cleothilda said, speaking in the deep, soft, straining tone of an old car climbing Calvary Hill in first gear. 'And if was one thing you could depend on was the equalness of everybody . . . Eh, Olive? Eh?'

'Maybe,' Miss Olive said, 'somebody had a pot or two or a dress or two more than you; but everybody was one.'

'Not that we didn't have ambition,' Cleothilda said, 'but nobody here look at things as if things is everything. If you had more money, you buy more food; and if is a holiday, you buy drinks for your friends, and everybody sit down and drink it out, and if tomorrow you ain't have none, you know everybody done had a good time, and all of we was. . .'

'One,' Miss Olive filled in into the pause, shaking a triumphant index finger at the city. 'If a man had money he didn't go and buy things to show off. You, Miss Cleothilda, you buy nice curtains and you have radio and furnitures, but I don't call that showing off – you always had them. It ain't something that you buy, just to show off.'

'Who?' Miss Cleothilda asked, 'who in this yard like to show off?'

'We come and meet you with what you have, I don't call that showing off,' Olive said.

'Not a soul in this yard like to show off,' Miss Cleothilda cried, her voice hoarse now as if she had been screaming all day. 'You feel Aldrick can't buy a bicycle if he want to? You feel you, Miss Olive, if you really want a bike – really want one . . .'

'What I goin' do with bike, Miss Cleothilda?' Miss Olive asked, scandalized at the very thought.

Aldrick stifled his smile as he tried to imagine Miss Olive on a bicycle going down Calvary Hill.

'No,' Miss Cleothilda said. 'I mean, you a little on the big side, is true, but if you really want to buy a bike, you can't save and save and buy one, you can't scrape and pinch and sell your soul to get one to show off with like the Indian boy do? But, bike have it people. Bike is not for you.'

'I see the little Indian fellar with his basket o' channa,' Miss Olive said regretfully, softly, in her hurt, 'I say "good morning", I say "good evening". I say "Howde do". He so quiet and he wife too. Who coulda imagine he was dangerous so?'

'Next thing he will want is to open a parlour,' Miss Cleothilda said.

'No!' Miss Olive cried. 'No!'

'No? If in . . . in how much? If in two years he could buy a bike, why he can't open a parlour?'

Miss Olive was silent, staggered, no doubt, by the thought, and she turned towards Aldrick as if he alone could save them, even as Miss Cleothilda, her voice filled with a jubilant gravity, was saying: 'I don't see how we could have him living here in this yard. Eh, Aldrick? Eh? You not saying nutten at all.'

Aldrick was sure now that it was not by accident that this conversation was being carried on in his presence. The Yard had already chosen him as the one to defend it against the Indian; for it was he, more than Guy or Philo, who most faithfully upheld that living, that code; who, indeed, lived the reality of non-possession as a way of life that Pariag in acquiring the bicycle was now violating.

Earlier it would have thrilled him to provide in violence an answer to Pariag's audacity, but now he felt that he did not want to be hurried into anything. He was not sure any more about a lot of things. He wasn't so sure that to buy a bicycle was such a sacrilege; and as his mind closed on this treason, he threw his towel over his shoulder, picked up his soap, and started to move away.

'Aldrick, you not saying nothing?' Miss Olive demanded, her hushed voice already husbanding the outrage, the scandal that such a thing had happened and it hadn't moved him.

'Only in this yard this thing could happen,' Miss Cleothilda said as if she was regretting that she wasn't a man with muscles.

Aldrick could feel the eyes of the women on him, and, as he went past them, slowly, with a nonchalant crawl, he turned and smiled, giving to his face what he imagined to be a sneering evil look that announced: 'I am still Aldrick; I am still the Dragon on Calvary Hill.' But even as he engaged in this uneasy fiction, he felt hurried, he felt in need of time. He resented that they had taken it for granted that he would move madly against the Indian fellar, without a pause to think things over, without a question; and his resentment would have more fuel for its fire as the week went on, for every day Miss Cleothilda positioned herself in such a way as to be present whenever he came into the Yard, so she could say to him, in salutation and warning and surprise, 'Good morning, Aldrick!' to which he smiled and tried to look tough.

He could feel the Yard, growing suspicious of him. Miss Olive, when he passed her, was always sitting on her front steps, her two hands propping up her chin, following him with her eyes so intently as if it was only by the greatest act of will that she kept herself from openly accusing him. He didn't worry about that much. He felt he had lived too long among them, had been too faithfully the dragon, for them to make too great a treason of his hesitation. Soon, though, he would begin to worry.

Faithfully, every year, a few days before Carnival Monday, the fellars of the neighbourhood would come to his room to see his costume as he was putting the finishing touches on it; and he would send for a bottle of rum, and they would all sit down and talk, Philo and Sammy and Rio and fellars from Mr Alphonso shoemaker shop. They would sit down and talk about old times – Carnival, dragons – and soon somebody would start singing a calypso, and others would join in, and somebody would start to beat bottle and spoon, and one of the men, not Aldrick, would begin to do a dragon dance and, hearing the noise, the children from the street would come into the Yard, and soon they would be dancing too and Aldrick and the fellars would go out in the Yard and watch the children dance the dragon dance, and all the people from the Yard – Miss Olive and Caroline and Cleothilda too would come out to watch, and one of the fellars would say, 'Aldrick, let us see you dance the dragon,' and he would say, 'No. You can't see me dance that dance; that is a secret.' And they would urge him again, and by that time the bottle would be finished and Mr Alphonso or Philo or Guy, if he was there, would send for another bottle, and when the bottle came they would drink again, and the children would be dancing, and he would see the little children dancing and looking at him for his admiration, for they knew that he was the king dragon, and he knew all the moves of the dragon dance, and he would say, 'Okay! Okay! Okay!' pointing to one of the children, 'let me see how good you is.' And the child would step forward, if he was brave, and if he was not, another – a brave one – would come out, and the men would start to sing louder and the music would get hotter, and the child would be opposite him, and they would dance, like they were having a contest, each one showing off his moves, each one showing off his beauty, and pretty soon everybody would join in, and the whole Yard would be singing and dancing.

There was no set day for this to take place, and though it was usually a day or two before Carnival, it just happened: a feeling just came over everybody and they said, 'Let's go by Aldrick today,' and they came and the thing took place. It was just as if the day chose itself, and people came. But it was Thursday now, and Aldrick knew that nobody was coming. They were waiting to see what he would do to the Indian. So when he heard the sound of approaching foot-steps as he sat in his room, half way figuring that they might still come, he knew that it was not one of the regular men. He was hoping it would be Sylvia, but when he turned, and he had delayed his turning, pretending to be absorbed in the dragon costume, so that she would have to speak first in order to turn him around – and even then he still didn't know what he would say – when he turned, it was Mr Guy, his face serious and his forehead pleated, and though he had come to a standstill, for apparently he had reached his destination, he was still carrying about him that air of importance and hurry, as if even as he was making this visit he was feeling that he ought to have been elsewhere.

'Prospect!' Guy said, calling him by his surname, the better to confirm the superiority he was seeking to estab-lish in his tone, a tone already possessing an edge of censure, as if it had been contrived to push Aldrick back on the defensive, to rob him of that self-possessed cool with which he seemed to wait on every situation. 'The Indian buy a bike!' And having made the announcement, Guy folded his arms across his chest with that wonderful sense of self-righteousness and vindication, as if he had come simply to bear witness to the fulfilling of a prophecy which he himself had made.

'He buy a bike?' Aldrick asked, his own tone calm, patient, his voice soft.

'Brand new Humber,' Guy said triumphantly. 'How you like that?'

'How you want me to like it?'

Guy grunted. He was a stocky, black complexioned man, and he made it a duty to be always neat and clean, to have his shirt pressed and well tucked into his trousers, his face shaved, his hair well parted, and a bit of cologne dabbed behind his ears and under his chin. He wore his neatness and cleanness as a compensation, so that the world would say: 'He black, but he never dirty.' 'How I expect you to like it?' Guy mused over the impertinence of the reply. 'No. You tell me how you expect me to expect you to like it. You tell me! Just now he will be buying a car, and after that a shop. . . . Just now he will own this whole street. You tell me how you like that.'

'How you like my dragon?' Aldrick asked, getting up and pushing open the door so that Guy could see it better.

'Very nice . . . very nice. Sit down there and ask me how I like your dragon . . . your dragon is very nice, Mr Prospect. Very nice.' Guy stood there shaking his head quickly, waiting, it seemed, for Aldrick to feel the weight of his sarcasm, and when Aldrick said nothing: 'You don't care if he take over the whole Hill, the whole town, as long as you play your masquerade, eh? You don't care.'

'Listen!' Aldrick said, his voice rising from its softness, recognizing Guy's audacity, giving off its own warning, 'Listen! Listen!'

'Anyhow,' Guy interrupted, 'you's your own man. You do what you want. I ain't come here to tell you what you must do. The rent! The house rent, that's what I come for. Let the Indian take over Alice Street . . . You have the rent? The owner in my backside all the time, you know. People think I own these buildings. They feel I own them. The owner in my arse every day for his money.'

'What about the rent?' Aldrick asked, pushing back the swinging door against the wind.

'What about the rent? Today is the tenth – that's what

about the rent. The month end ten days ago. That's what about the rent.'

'You have to give me a chance this month, Mr Guy. . . . Carnival . . . I have to make my costume. You know how much this dragon cost me?'

'Your dragon! You want me to go and tell the owner about your dragon?'

'You will have to give me a chance this month.'

'Chance? What chance you want me to give you again? The owner tell me, "No more chance!" The owner say to give you-all, all of you, notice to leave if you don't pay. Give you a chance? The Indian living here two years, you think he ever one month ask for a chance? Eh?'

'Listen!' Aldrick said, his tone hardening. 'Listen, I ain't have no rent today. Okay? I don't have it. Is nine years I living here, I can't owe you some rent?'

'How much rent you want to owe? Eh? Is ten months, man. Is ten months you ain't pay no rent, or, you forget? What you want me to tell the owner?'

'Okay, ten months. Okay. I going somewhere? Eh? Every day you get up and look out, you see me here, not so? You think I going away to America or somewhere tomorrow morning? Eh? Well, what the hell you rushing me so for, this big Carnival week? When I get the money I will pay.' Aldrick came out and sat on his steps. He was tapping his feet. 'Well, what the hell going on in this place? What it is? I must be getting soft or something. I must be getting old. First they come fucking up my brain about the Indian; now this man come telling me about rent.' He stood up in front of Guy. 'Listen, man, I is still Aldrick. I is still the dragon. I could turn beast in a minute!'

'That is what I say,' Guy said in a more polite tone, taking a step backward. 'The Indian must take over this place. You have your masquerade to play, so you can't think 'bout nutten else. How you like that? How you like that?' Guy gave a short, tight laugh, turned and walked away, leaving Aldrick seething there, regretting that he hadn't cuffed Guy in his mouth from the very beginning.

So he was ready to jump when Philo came by later: 'Don't tell me you come to tell me that the Indian buy a bike too. Don't . . .' And before the surprised Philo could get in a word, 'Don't tell me that they send you to advise me what to do. What you want me to do? Kill him? Mash up his bicycle? What you want me to do?'

'Wait!' Philo cried. 'Wait! Hold it!'

'No. What the hell happen with everybody? I know Cleothilda put a lotta shit in your head. I know, so don't tell me you don't know what I talking about. Everybody behind me to attack the Indian. Well, let me tell you something . . .'

'Me? But I ain't say nothing,' Philo said. 'I come here to . . .'

'No. Let me tell you anyway. You see me here, I is thirty-one years old. Never had a regular job in my life or a wife or nutten. I ain't own house or car or radio or race-horse or store. I don't own one thing in this fucking place, except that dragon there, and the dragon ain't even mine. I just make it. It just come out of me like a child who ain't really his father own or his mother own . . . They killing people in this place, Philo. Little girls, they have them whoring. And I is a dragon. And what is a man? What is you or me, Philo? And I here playing a dragon, playing a masquerade every year, and I forget what I playing it for, what I trying to say. I forget, Philo. Is like nobody remember what life is, and who we fighting and what we fighting for . . . Everybody rushing me as if they in such a hurry. I want to catch a breath, I want to see what I doing, to try to remember what life is and who is I and what I doing on this fucking Hill. Let the Indian buy his bike. Guy and Cleothilda ain't fooling me. The Indian is a threat to them, he ain't no threat to me.'

'I didn't come here to talk about the Indian, you know. I come for us to go and take a drink and for you to listen to a new calypso. I don't want to get in no controversy.'

'Get in the controversy, man. Get in. You in it already.'

'I watching and listening, that is all,' Philo said. 'But, you don't find it funny, this Indian. He off by himself, he and he wife. You don't know what going on with them, then sudden so he appear with a brand new bicycle. It strange, you know. People don't live so on the Hill.'

'How people does live? Cleothilda with she parlour, doing what she like when she like, don't care 'bout nobody; Guy collecting he rent, buying up property, and trying to fuck all the little girls on the Hill. How we does live? I, grinning and spinning, I can't talk straight to a man, I can't answer a question from a girl; I don't know how to deal with a boy who ain't have no home . . . They put Fisheye out the band, you know. Sponsors coming in; they don't want no more bad Johns. How we does live, Philo? Guy and Cleothilda trying to protect what they own.'

'What they own? How much they own?'

'I not a arse, you know. I know they don't own Trinidad and Tobago, but the little they have they frighten the Indian come and give them competition. That must threaten them. The rest of us ain't threatening them at all. All we thinking about is to play dragon. All we thinking about is to show this city, this island, this world, that we is people, not because we own anything, not because we have things, but because we is. We are because we is. You know what I mean?'

'This girl really set you thinking, man. I tell you . . . I tell you . . . Have your head on! Have your head on! But, I really ain't come to talk about the Indian, I come to let us take a drink and listen to this new calypso I going to sing tonight . . . You going? Le' we go to Freddie's snackette. They have a back room there where we could sit down.'

'Okay!'

Soon after he got to Freddie's, he wished he hadn't gone at all. All it did was to make him feel much sadder and to get him drunker than he wanted to be; but later, thinking it over, it struck him that the very sadness he felt then was part of coming to grips with what was really happening to the people on the Hill, and this knowledge would begin to point him to what he would learn more fully later on: that he had to bear alone, and without the luxury of any friend or company, the burden of his own living.

The Axe Man was the name of Philo's new calypso. They sat in the back room of Freddie's snackette, over a flask of rum, and Aldrick listened to him sing it.

It was one of those suggestive calypsos – filled with phallic symbolism and sexual overtones – was, rather, a simple metaphor of male sexual conquest, and when Philo sang it in the tent later that very evening he would get three encores for it. And patrons in the front seat would throw dollar bills on to the stage.

The story was about the very best axe man in the island. He went all over the country, cutting down trees that other axe men had failed to fell, until he met a tree that blunted his axe and forced him to take it to the hospital to have it repaired. This was the chorus:

> *I am the axe man cutting forests down*
> *I am the axe man working all over town*
> *If you have a tree to cut, I am the man to call*
> *I never put my axe on a tree and it didn't break and fall.*

'You don't like it, eh?' Philo had asked uneasily, when he had completed it.

And Aldrick had sat very silently, not even sipping the rum, shaking his glass, watching the ice spin and melt and turn the liquid to a lighter brown.

'Is okay if you don't like it, man. Is just something new I trying.' And when no word: 'You could tell me how you like it . . . I know you must be saying that I change, that this is not my style, my kinda song, that I ain't protesting again, I ain't singing against the bad things in the place. But, man, you have to sing what the people want to hear.'

'Yeh,' Aldrick said. 'Yeh!'

'Man, year in year out, I singing about how people hungry, how officials ain't doing their duty, and what I get, man? What I get? I want to win the Calypso King crown, at least reach the finals this year, one year, so I could say after this whole thing finish. "I was there".'

'So you could say what?'

'So that people would write down my name, man. So my name could be somewhere.'

'Yeh,' Aldrick said. 'Yeh!'

'It don't mean I don't care, or that I give up the battle . . . you understand, man. It don't mean I surrender. I is forty-two you know.'

'I understand, man,' Aldrick said. 'Yeh.' And indeed he understood too well: it was like everybody was suddenly getting jumpy; everybody was hustling to be somebody, to get something, get somewhere in a hurry. It was like everybody, people, felt they were running out of time, and they had to have something to show for being here. People were losing patience with the promise, with the hope, with the dreams, with the battle.

'You really understand, Aldrick?'

'Yeh, I tell you. Yeh.'

Aldrick drank off in one swig the drink in his glass, even though it was mostly water, and he sat back in his chair, looking so tired and in need of cheering that Philo felt moved to say: 'Is that Sylvia, man. Not so? If I had the money I'd give you to get that costume for her.'

The girl had come to his mind then, though she had been part of the complex of things filling it all evening. 'She must get that costume by now,' he said. 'Carnival is just three days away.'

Philo had to go to sing at the tent that night, so Aldrick remained there over another flask that Philo had paid for before he left. He remained there at Freddie's snackette drinking rum, listening to the juke box blare out calypso after calypso, watching men and women dancing, not holding on to each other, beginning already the abandon,

the surrender that marked Carnival. He could understand
Philo; but then again, he couldn't understand him. He
thought about Sylvia.

She must get that costume by now, he thought.

Next morning, waking with a headache from the rum (his
head was getting weak for rum) he was still thinking it, as a
continuing thought that would flit endlessly through his
brain in its waking: she must get her costume by now. He
was afraid to look outside and have his suspicion confirmed.

He was still sitting on the edge of the bed, the one clear
phrase, fear, announcement, repeating itself in his brain,
as he looked at the head of the dragon hanging on the wall,
the eyes, saw through the eyes, past the eyes, beyond the
eyes to his own loneliness, his own tiredness, and his
mind thinking about Sylvia, crying for the lost dragons, for
Philo and Fisheye, for himself even, so that when the
knock sounded on the door, it startled him. He had
thought himself alone, and the knock seemed to enter past
the closed door to uncover him in his posture of aloneness
and bewilderment and pain, so that already, without knowing who was at his door, he was snapping: 'Who the hell is
that?'

It was Pariag.

'I disturbing you?' Pariag asked, testingly.

'Man, I now getting up,' Aldrick answered, without
going to the door.

'Well, is nothing much. I . . . I could come back.'

'Okay! Okay, what it is? You here already.' Aldrick went
to the door.

'Well, I know you could paint, so I was wondering if you
could paint a sign on a box for me. I have the words right
here.' He had a sheet of paper in his hand and he gave it to
Aldrick. 'Is for the box I putting on my bicycle.'

Aldrick looked at the paper, then he looked at Pariag.

Aldrick read from the paper: "Boya for Indian Delicacies.
Barra and Doubles!!!" 'Where you say you want me to paint

this? What colours?' He rubbed his eyes. He didn't feel too good this morning. 'Why you don't come back later when I really wake up, eh?' And even as he was saying this he knew that he didn't want to sound too soft. He didn't want Pariag to feel that he was on his side.

'Okay,' Pariag said in his soft, wounded voice. 'Okay!' Aldrick had been his last desperate hope to become part of the Yard, at least to understand what evil he had done. He turned away, not even bothering to take the paper from Aldrick.

'Come back later,' Aldrick called, softening a little at the sight of the young man's soft, tall retreat.

Then he spotted her, Sylvia, a glimpse, a blur, moving in a terribly energetic hurry, sweeping out her door and turning towards the street, without casting an eye in any direction but the one she was heading in.

I sure she get her costume by now, he thought.

And then he felt a wave of emptiness, of pain with holes, roll across all his insides. He held on to the two posts of the doorway.

'Fuck it!' he whispered.

7   Norman 'Tex' at the Carnival Fête

On Carnival Saturday night, he had got over it, he thought, fêting at Legion Hall with Philo and Reggie and another calypsonian named Bomb, and four *jamette* women. It was a great fête. The bands playing, Trinidad All Stars Steelband, and Norman 'Tex' Williams. And, Norman 'Tex' was hot. This was their season, their time. This was their night: they was ripe. They was ready.

They had a fast beat, a not exactly calypso beat, a kinda rock-swing, old bee-bop slowed down, kinda like a hallelujah humming in the background at a Baptist meeting while the tune going on up front where the preacher preaching; and they was taking classic tunes, tunes like lieberstraum and intermezzo and barcarole, and threading them through with calypso, swinging them and mocking them and quarrelling with them and opening their bellies and bringing out the soul in them, to have you dancing and listening and crying and trying to reach yourself, trying to touch a time and a girl who you used to see by the corner walking down the road prim and proper and you frighten to talk to her, to say good morning to her, lest you melt away if she don't answer, and you praying to meet her in a dance so you could go up to her and say, 'Miss may I have this dance with you,' but you will never meet her, you will never see her anywhere but walking down the street prim and proper, and you without the courage to open your mouth and say good morning to her. These tunes bring her back to you; so now, this night, with these tunes, you kinda looking around in the smoke-filled room trying to see if you could see her, these tunes that long after you leave the dance hall you find yourself whistling just so, remembering again the girl by the corner, and you don't know that you did hear 'Tex' Williams play them one night, that night. And that night 'Tex' was, as the advertisement on the LP record that he would cut later proclaimed, in a rage. Joe Sampson, a tall, baby-faced boy with a long-sleeved shirt on, was on the guitar; and Alvin Albino was playing the piano; and Norman 'Tex' was blowing the saxophone like he wanted to blow into it not only the air from his body, but all the organs of his own life; and he was blowing, blowing, the veins on his neck straining, and a knot forming on his forehead and his eyes popping out his head, and holding his lips to the saxophone as if he really done blow out his insides into it and can't afford for it to slip from his lips before the tune finish, else he would drop dead, since all his insides, his heart and liver and lungs and everything inside the saxophone. That was fête! Everybody was sweet, was nice, and the women they had with them was drinking and smoking and laughing and taking you up to dance, and sometimes they would link their arms, the six of them, and make a ring round a dancing couple and dance, jump-up, leggo. The table was right near the band, so when people came to stand up and gaze at the musicians they would see them. Philo was suddenly popular with his Axe Man calypso and people was calling out to him and to Bomb who was a singer in the Young Brigade Calypso Tent too: 'Wha' happenin', Philo!' 'Wha' happenin', Bomb?' And there were some who knew Reggie and Aldrick and they would say, 'Come and meet some friends and take one,' and they would introduce them around: 'This is Reggie, this is Inez, and Rita, and Claire,' and he forgot the name of the other girl, and 'This is Aldrick, the greatest dragon in town, in the world.' And the people would say, 'Pleasetomeet you', though in the smoke and the noise and the lights low you couldn't make out nobody and you couldn't hear nutten but the music.

That was fète! They had a good time, everybody; and Philo and his girl was drinking Guinness stout, and two fellars and the girls was drinking scotch, and only he alone was drinking rum. He had forgotten her, Sylvia, with the rum and the noise and the smoke and everybody talking and he was so cool that he got up and went over and stood up and watched the little Sampson boy play his guitar. He was cool, and his face serious, and not making any fuss, like if he wasn't playing at all, like it was easy, like if you put a long-sleeved shirt and close your eyes and stand up with your head cocked to one side, you could do it too, but Aldrick was watching his fingers how they was moving. And all the time Norman 'Tex', writhing and straining and bending back from his waist, from his knees, from his ankles, his two hands stretched out pressing the sax to his lips, his face twisted up in this pain, this pain, this pain, and wanting to blow a note, the note, to blow it out, and already kinda half-knowing he would never get the note to blow, but, same time feeling, 'Now! Now I have it! I going to blow it now!', and stretching over the saxophone and twisting and turning, dancing to the same music he trying to blow, in a slow pain, with this tall note like a child in the womb of a woman's pain, he trying to blow, his shoulders hunched over and trembling and his eyes watching his lips; and the baby-faced Sampson boy cool, his fingers moving over the guitar face, his feet tapping, his lips mumbling like he shame to talk to the guitar in front all these strange people, and Albino, watching sideways and hitting the piano keys, turning every now and again to see if the rest of the band still there or if is he alone playing.

Afterwards, with morning coming on, and the wind blowing cool and man looking for woman to go home with, he sat down on the concrete flooring in the Yard, with Inez holding him round his shoulders, and Philo and Reggie and Bomb all wrapped up with their women, and then it touched him – she must get her costume by now – lanced him, like an old wound that for a moment he had forgotten, slicing through him in a sweet, twisting, hurting ache, and same time Philo signalled to him that he was going home with his woman, and he nodded his head, 'okay'; and he sat down there with Inez pressing closer to him as the cool wind blew – and nobody didn't want to drink again – half tired and kinda peaceful and her knees together. Her dress had slipped up a little to expose the frilly edge of her slip and more of her thigh, and he thought of it, of how it would be at five o'clock in the morning after all that dancing and rum and scotch and Guinness, and he let his hand slip down her thigh where her slip was showing, and she didn't say nothing, and he said: 'You sleepy? Let's take a taxi and go home.' Afterwards, in the midst of moving with her, their naked bodies locked together in a wonderful striving, it had come back again, the hurt, slower and more lasting, and he had grown gentle with her and he had kissed her softly.

'Haii!' she said. 'What happen?'

'You nice,' he said.

She was silent for a while, then she kissed him on his cheek, with a kind of grateful gentleness. After that they just lay close to each other and talked until they dropped off to sleep.

8   To Be Dragon and Man

Up on the Hill Carnival Monday morning
breaks upon the backs of these thin shacks with no cock's
crow, and before the mist clears, little boys, costumed in
old dresses, their heads tied, holding brooms made from
the ribs of coconut palm leaves, blowing whistles and
beating kerosene tins for drums, move across the face of
the awakening Hill, sweeping yards in a ritual, heralding
the masqueraders' coming, that goes back centuries for its
beginnings, back across the Middle Passage, back to Mali
and to Guinea and Dahomey and Congo, back to Africa
when Maskers were sacred and revered, the keepers of the
poisons and heads of secret societies, and such children
went before them, clearing the ground, announcing their
coming to the huts before which they would dance and
make their terrible cries, affirming for the village, the
tribe, warriorhood and femininity, linking the villagers to
their ancestors, their Gods, remembered even now, so long
after the Crossing, if not in the brain, certainly in the
blood; so that every Carnival Monday morning, Aldrick
Prospect, with only the memory burning in his blood, a
memory that had endured the three hundred odd years to
Calvary Hill felt, as he put on his dragon costume, a sense
of entering a sacred mask that invested him with an ancestral authority to uphold before the people of this Hill, this
tribe marooned so far from the homeland that never was
their home, the warriorhood that had not died in them,
their humanness that was determined not by their
possession of things. He had a desire, a mission, to let

them see their beauty, to uphold the unending rebellion they waged, huddled here on this stone and dirt hill hanging over the city like the open claws on a dragon's hand, threatening destruction if they were not recognized as human beings.

But this Carnival, putting on his costume now at dawn, Aldrick had a feeling of being the last one, the last symbol of rebellion and threat to confront Port of Spain. Fisheye was under orders not to misbehave, Philo had given up on his own calypsos of rebellion to sing now about the Axe Man. Once upon a time the entire Carnival was expressions of rebellion. Once there were stickfighters who assembled each year to keep alive in battles between themselves the practice of a warriorhood born in them; and there were devils, black men who blackened themselves further with black grease to make of their very blackness a menace, a threat. They moved along the streets with horns on their heads and tridents in hand. They threatened to press their blackened selves against the well dressed spectators unless they were given money. And there were the jab jabs, men in jester costumes, their caps and shoes filled with tinkling bells, cracking long whips in the streets, with which they lashed each other with full force, proclaiming in this display that they could receive the hardest blow without flinching at its coming, without feeling what, at its landing, must have been burning pain. Suddenly they were all gone, outlawed from the city or just died, gone, and he felt alone. The dragon alone was left to carry the message. He felt that now, alone, with even Philo and Fisheye gone, it was too great to carry. It would be lost now among the clowns, among the fancy robbers and the fantasy presentations that were steadily entering Carnival; drowned amidst the satin and silks and the beads and feathers and rhinestones. But bothering him even more than this was the thought that maybe he didn't believe in the dragon any more.

The moment Aldrick stepped outside, Carnival hit him.

And his heart grew big, and he felt a softness flow over him, and the burning of tears in his nostrils; for there before him on the street, the steelband and masqueraders were assembling. The months of practising and sewing and painting and building were flowing together in the stillness of the morning under the eyes of women and children who had awakened from sleep and dressed hurriedly to come out and watch their band, to see their people, to admire them and to cheer them and to accompany them, to tramp the pavement, while the masqueraders occupied the street, as a sort of guard, right into Port of Spain. It hit him: masqueraders stepping out of these red dirt and stone yards, through the doors of leaning wooden shacks, middle-aged ladies fixing their brassiere straps, old man Johnson and his three grandchildren coming out as robbers, Prince, dressed up as a fancy Indian, showing off his headpiece, turning delicately, the breeze rocking him, so the people could see it, so they could say, 'Hey, Prince! Man, you looking good. Man, you looking sweet. You go kill them.' It hit him, the red and black and gold and green, the colours and the feathers and the satin, and the people's faces with that look in their eyes, and the smell of cologne and face powder, and the smell of grease and the look of wonder on children's faces, and the little fellars with sailor caps on and round-necked jerseys without no print, looking at the steelbandsmen lifting their pans onto the street, setting them down gently on the asphalt surface to a thrilling, scraping, metallic sound; and what reverence, what awe as if they alone in the whole world had the real eyes to see the real thing, to see heroes, to see giants, gods. And these little fellars waiting for the band to get underway so they could glide up to the steeldrums and touch one, or wave to a brother or cousin who was playing one of the pans, or help the men push the stands on which the big steel drums were mounted.

And watching, fascinated by it all, as if he were seeing with the boys' eyes, Aldrick felt a tallness and a pride, felt his hair rise on his head, felt: 'No, this ain't no joke. This is warriors going to battle. This is the guts of the people, their blood; this is the self of the people that they screaming out they possess, that they scrimp and save and whore and work and thief to drag out of the hard rockstone and dirt to show the world they is people.' He felt: 'This is people taller than cathedrals; this is people more beautiful than avenues with trees.' And full to brimming with furious tears, Aldrick felt again the fierce love and hope that he had doubted in himself, felt again a sense of mission; felt that yes, there was a place here for him, that there was something to say yes to, and people before whom and on whose behalf he could dance the dragon. With a strong, piercing scream, he stepped into the street, his chains rattling, his arms outflung, his head lolling, in a slow, threatening dance of the Beast, so that the people of the Hill turned to him, recognizing him, said, 'Yes! Yes! That is Dragon!'

Afterwards Terry rang a piece of iron, calling the band to attention; then, One . . . two . . . three . . . four, Pram! The music burst forth from the steelband; shouts went up, and the steelband and the masqueraders and the women who had come to watch and the little boys waiting to venture to touch a pan and the help to push the stands and the robbers and the Indians and the clowns – the whole Hill began moving down upon Port of Spain.

For two full days Aldrick was a dragon in Port of Spain, moving through the loud, hot streets, dancing the bad-devil dance, dancing the stickman dance, dancing Sylvia and Inez and Basil and his grandfather and the Hill and the fellars by the Corner, leaning against the wall, waiting for the police to raid them. He was Manzanilla, Calvary Hill, Congo, Dahomey, Ghana. He was Africa, the ancestral Masker, affirming the power of the warrior, prancing and bowing, breathing out fire, lunging against his chains, threatening with his claws, saying to the city: 'I is a dragon. I have fire in my belly and claws on my hands; watch me! Note me well, for I am ready to burn down your city. I am ready to tear you apart, limb by limb.'

And he watched terror strike pale faces as he lunged towards them, and he smiled inwardly as they grinned nervously and rushed hands into their pockets to find coins to offer him in appeasement, as was the tradition. But no. No. He refused the money. He wanted it to be known that he was for real, that you couldn't just offer him a coin and he would disappear. He wanted them to know that he would always be threatening there, a breath away from them. Some couldn't understand it, this refusal of the coins. They thought that they were not offering enough; and as he danced before them they made another journey into their pockets and showed him more coins. He didn't take the money – 'No, this couldn't happen! This dragon was crazy! This fellar wanted trouble!' But it was Carnival. Whoever heard someone calling the police for a Dragon. Aldrick growled and he spat and he moved to press against them, watched them grow more afraid, more confused. He wanted to frighten them. He liked it when they saw him coming and gathered up their children and ran.

Oh, he danced. He danced pretty. He danced to say, ' You are beautiful, Calvary Hill and John John and Laventille and Shanty Town. Listen to your steelbands how they playing! Look at your children how they dancing! Look at your beads and feathers! Look at the colours of your costumes in the sunshine! Look at your colours! You is people, people. People is you, people!' He wanted everybody to see him. When they saw him, they had to be blind not to see. They had to be deaf not to hear that people everywhere want to be people, and that they going to be that anyway, even if they have to rip open the guts of the city.

And he wasn't even tired when he started to see people hurrying down Charlotte Street to get buses and trains to take them home: mothers gathering children, vendors dismantling stalls, couples sitting on the pavement in each other's arms, or masqueraders simply sprawled full length across the sidewalk sound asleep. He wasn't even tired yet and he saw the homeward trek and the darkness coming down; and then he felt he would like to sit down. And then he thought, 'If I could just make it to the Corner where the Calvary Hill band passing to go home, that would be boss.'

When he reached the Corner of Calvary Hill and Observatory Street he said: 'Yes,' and he sat down on the pavement. Suddenly the head of the dragon on his neck weighed a ton, and he unhooked the head and rested it on the ground beside him and wiped his face with a handkerchief and watched the Carnival ending; masqueraders, so splendidly dressed earlier in the day, moving across the streets leaving a trail of bits and pieces of their costumes, dragging their swords and spears and banners, going home now, leaving it now. And he thought, Aldrick thought: 'You know, tomorrow is no Carnival.' And he understood then what it meant when people said that they wished every day was Carnival. For the reign of kings and princesses was ending, costumes used today to display the selves of people were going to be taken off. What of those selves? What of the selves of these thousands? What of his own self?

Aldrick took out the flask of rum from the pocket he had sewn at the joining in the dragon's tail. It still had a shot in it, and he drank it in one. He felt like a coke or a drink of water, but the stall across the street seemed a thousand miles away, and he didn't see anybody he could ask to go get a coke or a drink of water for him; he drained the flask of its last few drops of rum. He bowed his head onto his chest to just rest a little, and next thing he knew was waking from this nice, sweet sleep, not really waking fully, but being aware that he was sleeping this wonderful sleep, hearing at the same time far away all the sounds of the two days, seeing the colours and the movement of limbs, smelling the powder and the sweat and the stale perfume.

Then, strum! strum! strum! far in his ears he heard the steelband beating, and when he opened his eyes he could see, coming round the corner, the Calvary Hill band.

He watched it come on, slow, with a beat, a basic strum, the iron starting and stopping and starting again and the bass drums grumbling. He watched it come on, slow, dragging, a tired dragon holding in its belly the whole Hill: spectators and masqueraders and steelbandsmen and supporters, women and children, Robbers and Indians and the bicycle stunt-man. Sylvia and another girl her own age were the eyes, alive, dancing still with that same furious spirit with which they began on Monday morning, dancing, as if they refused to accept the ending of Carnival and wanted in their dance, out of their own boundless energy and desiring, to call it back again. Miss Cleothilda was in it, with Philo holding her importantly round her waist, jumping up in her young-oldish way, trying to keep faith with a youth that was now deserting her – the spirit was willing, but the flesh . . . her feet could hardly leave the ground, and her head couldn't stay straight.

He sat there and let part of the band pass before him, then he made the effort, stood up, leaving the head of his dragon costume right there on the pavement, and joined the band going home now to a dragging beat, a slow strum, a going-home strum. The music was a bit raggedy, because not all the steelbandsmen were playing. Some of them now at the end of the day were taking time out to hug-up their women and cruise home with them, so there were only two tenors playing the melody, the rest was rhythm, the second pans and the guitar and the booms strumming, syncopating. And all the shouting and talking was at an end – it was just a quietness and this sweet, tired, slow strumming. Later he would learn that some of the steelbandsmen had been injured in a fight that took place earlier in the evening when they tried to subdue Fisheye who had gone crazy as the band was going up Henry Street and tried to mash up the pans. Seven of them were in hospital, as well as Fisheye and Reds.

Little by little Aldrick worked his way to the front of the band. Then he saw Sylvia, dancing still with all her dizzying aliveness, dancing wildly; frantically twisting her body, flinging it around her waist, jumping and moving, refusing to let go of that visibility, that self the Carnival gave her; holding it balanced on her swaying hips, going down and coming up in a tall, undulating rhythm, lifting up her arms and leaping as if she wanted to leap out of herself into her self, a self in which she could stay for ever, in which she could *be* for ever. He watched her dancing into the insides of the music, into the Carnival's guts, into its every note, its soul, into every ring of the tall ringing iron; her whole self a shout, a bawl, a cry, a scream, a cyclone of tears rejoicing in a self and praying for a self to live in beyond Carnival and her slave girl costume.

He watched her, perspiration flowing down her face, bursting onto her skin, drenching her costume; and he wanted to reach out and hold her, not to tame her to the truth that Carnival must soon end, but to join her in the tall, rejoicing dance, cry; to swirl with her in the cyclone of affirming tears, and lose himself and gain himself in her, swirling away with her until together they disappeared into the self that she was calling back, calling forth, praying for. He watched her. And in the face of this scream for life, this cyclone of affirming and appealing tears, it suddenly struck him that his dragon with its threatening claws and fire was small before this girl's scream. He wanted to give her life, her self. But, how could he?

He could threaten. He had to learn how to live and how to give life; this flash came to his brain, humbling him. And suddenly, he wanted to touch Sylvia, to tell her in his touching what had just been revealed to him. He found himself moving towards her, gliding through the spaces between the dancers to her side. 'Sylvia!' He reached out a hand to touch her, to receive her blessing and to bless her, to cheer her and to be cheered by her. And then she saw him, saw his awkward hand reaching to her, and in one movement she spun out of his reach and turned to face him in a tall, sweeping disdain.

'No, mister!' she said. 'I have my man!'

'You have your . . . your man?' he mumbled, and he felt a numbness close over him. 'You have your man?' And, looming up beside her in a white sailor suit was Guy: Guy, his grabbing hand closing around her bare waist as she moved close to him. He wanted to laugh, to ease himself of his embarrassment, but his muscles didn't work. He couldn't laugh. He really wanted to laugh, to make some gesture of uncaring, of superiority, but his body didn't move. He just stood there in the band and let the crowd move on around him, not even caring that they bounced him around. He stood not so much stubborn as seized, until he was all alone behind the band. Then he began to walk; each aching step, alone; a strange new torturing pain and sweetness in his soul, a kind of crazy new caring and respect for the girl and a kind of warrior's pride in himself that he had chosen her, Sylvia, in that very instant, to be his woman.

9   Ash Wednesday

Ash Wednesday morning is the wickedest day of the year on the Hill; and Aldrick, waking with thoughts of Sylvia and the steel and brass and colours of Carnival pounding in his brain, his neck and shoulders aching and all his limbs alive with pain from carrying around his dragon costume for the two full days of the festival, swung open his door upon the desolate noiselessness of the drowsy sunlit street where the beating hearts seemed to have been gouged out of things, leaving them drum-hollow, so that for an instant, in the half stupor of his awakening, the street seemed to be the very guts of emptiness, and the shacks, teetering on their rickety pillars, abandoned and condemned. And for the first time, he found in his nostrils the odour of poverty, the flat, dull odour, having the scent of stale water from a heavy washing that had remained still and unstirred for five or so days.

He remained there with one hand still holding the out-swung door, watching in a half-awake vacantness the Hill, in the sunlight, a brownish grey, silent corpse, without its music and its moving limbs; and it came to him now with a kind of amazement that this place was where he lived. This was home. These pathetic and ridiculous looking shacks planted in this brown dirt and stone, this was home. This was home. The thought waked him. This place was his home. He was going to laugh. And then he remembered the time when he was a boy, going to school in Port of Spain and living in Laventille. He carried lunch to school every day. All the children who lived a distance off carried lunch in little brown paper bags spotted with grease. His paper bag was always white or pink, and coloured with flowers or fancy designs, and some of them announced the name of a store: J. T. Johnstons, or Sabgas or advertised a product: Millway threads, Girlies stockings, so that it looked as if it did not contain food at all, but the finest lingerie, socks, thread, lace. Along with a piece of bake and saltfish or bread and accra, or whatever his mother could manage, he carried a bottle of tea brewed from wild-senna, a herb long sanctioned by his grandmother as a purifier of the blood. On weekends he drank it, boiled to the blackest green, as a laxative, and in the week it was brewed as tea. And because there was in the yard where they lived a wild-senna tree, when everything else ran out he would always have wild-senna tea.

Now he was not fond at all of this tea, but every day he went to school that year he found in his paper bag along with whatever else there was, a bottle of wild-senna tea, whitened with some condensed milk and sweetened. One lunchtime he opened his paper bag among his friends, and as he was about to take out his lunch, he was confronted by this one bottle of wild-senna tea. It was a *solo* bottle, a fat, round, chubby bottle. There was nothing else in the paper bag. Too late, he saw the boys looking at him, understanding and getting ready to ridicule his 'lunch'. He had stood there, he remembered now, looking at this 'lunch' of his, this white liquid, neither hot now nor cold, with one captured leaf of wild-senna afloat in the bottle.

He remembered one fellar asking, 'What's that?' and another answering with quick-witted mockery, 'That's his milk!' 'His milk? His milk?' And suddenly that solo bottle of wild-senna tea became the most wonderfully comical sight he had ever seen. It *was* funny. And he had laughed, he remembered, until his belly hurt; then he had seized the bottle which, magically now, by his laughter, had become distant from him, was now in a way no longer his own, no longer had the power to embarrass him, and had drunk it all down, right there in front the boys. They laughed, but their laughter didn't touch him.

All his life he had managed in such ways to disconnect himself from things which he couldn't escape and which threatened to define him in a way in which he didn't want to be defined, and go on untouched, untouched by things that should have touched him, hurt him, burned him. And that was why this hurting over Sylvia, even though he explained it to himself as love – love? – confused him. He had reached home last night with the phrase 'I have my man' hammering in his brain, hammering at his whole self, torturing him so that if he had been able to he would have cried, if he could have felt the extent of feeling that it called forth, he would have been happy to let himself be soaked by the pain. And he had said to himself in anguish: 'I have to learn to feel.'

And he was thinking this again now, standing at his open door, watching the shacks stacked like medieval shields of a disassembled army, realizing that he had never really lived here on this Hill, never embraced this place as home, never felt it to himself, to his bones. He had been living in the world of the dragon, avoiding and denying the full touch of the Hill. He had been cheating himself of the pain, of the love, of his living. He had been laughing here for seventeen years.

'I have to learn to feel,' he thought, thinking beyond Sylvia to his dead uncle – Uncle Freddie – who lived for fifteen years on the Hill in an old house, a shack, never planting a flower, discouraging any effort to beautify or repair the broken-down house suggested far more in-augurated by any of the women who shared his life with him, consoling them with his jolly remark: 'Take it easy. We soon going to leave this place.' He died there, with the old house falling down about him. Fifteen years, and not a flower planted nor a fence mended.

She have her man. He couldn't laugh at that. No, sir. But this morning he felt humble before his own feelings, and not so afraid of them. He wanted to call them to him, to feel them. He felt a great distance from himself, as if he had been living elsewhere from himself, and he thought that he would like to try to come home to himself; and even though it sounded like some kind of treason, he felt that at least it was the only way he could begin to be true to even the promise of the dragon to which he felt bound in some way beyond reason, beyond explanation, and which he felt had its own truth.

Aldrick stood on his steps and turned to hook the door. A breeze blew, and he smiled as he felt it on his cheeks, and he smiled again as he saw Miss Olive, whose movement now separated her from the landscape into which she and the tub from which she was presently rising, had been merged as she did her washing, grab hold of the hem of her skirt as it flew up to her knees in the wind. She said something unkind to the wind, pressed down her skirt and bent over her washing again with an accustomed patience.

He stood there, one hand on the latch of the unlatched door, watching this large, patient woman over her tub – and she would toil almost daily there, for she was taking in washing now. Carnival was two days only. For the rest of the year she would be neither masquerader nor spectator; she would be. Her life would go on, as his would go on. And that life counted for something, hers and his. That life in between Ash Wednesday and Carnival Monday morning, it counted for something. He felt a comradeship with her now, and he wanted to call out to her, to say some word that would cement this joining, but he had had no practice in such words. And he thought about that, standing there with his hand on the door latch in the silence and inactivity of Ash Wednesday morning.

And turning now, with a sadness, not unpleasant to his soul, to fix the wooden bracket into place, he saw, coming into the Yard, stepping past the governor plum tree, her silken black dress rustling about her knees, her rosary dangling below her prayer book, Miss Cleothilda, her head held high, her black lace veil parted in the middle of her face the better to reveal the blackened cross of ashes the priest had marked upon her forehead at Communion mass earlier that morning. Aldrick watched her sweep forth in her brisk, tall, quick-stepping breathlessness, holding herself in that audacious and pious grandeur, as if already serving warning that now, with Carnival done and her sins expiated (as witness thereof, the symbol of repentance and forgiveness, the black cross sketched upon her forehead) she was ready again to take up where she had left off when the Carnival season came in.

And even as he groaned in his wisdom, he saw Miss Olive lifting herself up from her washing, to say: 'Good morning, Miss Cleothilda!' and to say it again when she got no answer, even though it fell upon Miss Cleothilda to utter the first word of salutation, since she was coming into the Yard and Miss Olive was already there. But Miss Cleothilda marched on. As if anxious to re-affirm her position in the Yard, lest the wrong impression prevail too long after her relaxation for Carnival, she was already grumbling about a pile of dog shit she had nearly stepped in, and wondering aloud why the police didn't jail those people who, with their own children starving, insisted on keeping a band of stray dogs to bring filth and disease into the place, imposing upon Miss Olive, by some trick of association, the burden of explaining the presence of dog shit in the Yard, though she very well knew that Miss Olive did not own a dog. And in that instant during which Miss Olive stood, her shoulders heaving, her tortured face beyond a reply, Miss Cleothilda marched up the steps to her apartment where her own dog, scenting her approach, was frisking and yapping.

Miss Olive's huge frame trembled, her nostrils flared, and her eyes narrowed. She looked up the steps at the dis-appearing Cleothilda, as if she wanted to rush after her, grab her and strangle her. That lasted for one instant. The next moment she just shook her head in martyred resignation, 'Hm!' she sighed, 'Hm!' Turning now, her eyes sweeping the Yard to see if she had been observed in her shame, her eyes met Aldrick's, and she smiled a smile of martyrdom and knowing that threatened, Aldrick felt, to draw him in together with her; a smile that suggested that the two of them shared a knowledge of Miss Cleothilda's secrets that in some subtle backhanded fashion made them superior to her and accepting of her.

'Miss Cleothilda crazy, yes,' she said, her eyes holding Aldrick's, a half wise smile on her face.

'Cleothilda really crazy,' she said again, waiting, Aldrick knew, despite the scorn and toughness in her tone and her superior smile, for his nod to sanction and uphold her.

'No,' Aldrick heard himself saying, shouting almost. 'She ain't crazy.' And even as he saw Miss Olive's eyes widen and her shoulders fold and the hurt rush across her face, he found himself repeating, with more firmness and less alarm, 'She ain't crazy at all.'

'What you mean . . . ? What you mean she ain't crazy?' Miss Olive's voice deepened, and she drew herself up proudly to her full six foot. Not another word. She bent over her tub and resumed her washing.

'Now she vexed with *me*,' Aldrick muttered as he slipped the wooden bracket in place to hold the door, and turned inside.

But, he was learning; and he felt it; and he bore it. Later he would watch Miss Olive surrounded now by that air of proud sullenness, going about the Yard, a little less anxious to please anybody, wilfully intent, by a kind of stubbornness to uphold her dignity. There grew about her movements a slowness, a footdragging deliberateness, so that she seemed now to always need a second call to make her hear Miss Cleothilda's invitations, and even to these she took her own sweet time to respond.

It didn't take Miss Cleothilda long to discover that a new situation had begun to exist in the Yard, a situation that she felt threatened her position as 'queen'. It wasn't only Olive's sullenness; it was Pariag's continued presence; it was Aldrick failing still, two weeks after Carnival, to take any action against him; it was Philo's sudden rise in popularity as a calypsonian; and it was Sylvia. Sylvia had a man. Guy could buy her things, Guy could keep her in style, and, with her youth and looks and that wild something she possessed, if she became ambitious, the Yard could have a new 'queen'. Miss Cleothilda began making readjustments.

Aldrick and Pariag, she decided, were enemies, and she had nothing to tell either of them. But to Miss Olive, she began to soften her voice when talking, and to create these contrived, important things for them to discuss, sighing with her over Pariag's new bicycle, and the fact that Aldrick had not lifted a finger to give the Yard any justice, using her as a go-between to woo Sylvia into a friendship with her, since she wanted the girl close so that not only would she become party to her secrets but would be able to advise her and tame her and shape her into what she wanted. And, instead of openly insulting Philo who swaggered into the Yard now, with his silk shirts and his bright scarves and a white panama hat, she would turn her replies to his insistent questions into a kind of joke, so that while she retained the upper hand in the relationship, she was creating the impression that she could not only be human but feminine.

'What you going to do with a old woman like me, Philo?' she would ask, tending her plants on the verandah.

And undaunted, Philo would reply: 'I could water your garden.'

Or, she would say: 'You know, with all this talk you talking, I feel you more hot than sweet.'

'Try me,' from Philo.

It became an unreal joking between them – Miss Cleothilda gradually softening her parries to Philo's thrusts, until soon, although it wasn't Carnival, Philo had begun to ascend Miss Cleothilda's steps and sit down on her verandah and play with her dog.

Whether or not she intended it to go so far, this relationship struck up with Philo seemed to persuade people that she was human, since it suggested that she was woman, although nobody couldn't say for certain how far beyond the verandah Philo went, though there would be gossip, people saying, and thinking 'You can't know how far he go when the night come'; saying this exultantly, happy to believe that Philo had pierced the privacy of her bedroom, making it a triumph they were anxious to share with him, a triumph that removed Cleothilda from her pedestal and prepared them to give to her a new acknowledgement if not the same old respect – All o' we is one!

So it wasn't long before Miss Cleothilda had the Yard eating out her hands again, so much so in fact, that Miss Olive was willing to concede to Miss Caroline one day: 'She not so bad, you know, Caroline. You just have to understand her moods.' Of course, by that time, Miss Olive had stopped talking to Aldrick; and, as to Pariag, whenever she saw him pushing his bicycle through the Yard she would let out a long steups.

One day Aldrick saw Pariag riding by with his new bicycle with his box with the delicacies he was supposed to be selling atop it. The box had been painted with the sign: 'Boya for Best Indian delicacies', the letters in red and blue, and a few yellow dots that looked like flowers in between the lettering. Pariag seemed cold. He wondered what would have happened if he had painted the sign. Maybe the Yard would have definitely concluded that they had some conspiracy going. Maybe it was better so, not painting the sign. Pariag's coldness was not so hurtful; they had never been friends, really at all. It made him feel more innocent, in a way cleaner, more pure, before the silent accusation of the Yard.

In truth, Aldrick felt the estrangement with the Yard. For all the years he had lived there, he had been the dragon, the king, setting the pace, living the style, and although in looking back now he felt that he had been living a dream from which he had recently awakened and found that he alone was real, that the others were still in that dream, he missed being a favourite, he missed passing down the street and fellars calling him for a drink, or stopping him just to talk to, and he missed having the freedom to call anyone and to drink any man's rum, and to enter any company on the Hill. A shyness had come over him, and though he still went to the gambling club and, on Sundays, to the all fours game at Mr Alphonso shoemaker shop, it was as if he carried a silence with him, so that as soon as he arrived all the gaiety seemed to go out of conversations. Even with Philo, who now that he was on top of the world, carried a new spirit that matched his silk shirts and coloured scarves, there were long periods of silence which Philo, charitably, chose not to notice, commenting after such moments, 'You shoulda buy the costume for her.'

Sylvia was always in his eyes. He would see her now, walking long-limbed, with that wonderful, soft drowsiness about her, as if she had just waked from sleep, dressed still in those silky, clingy nightgowny things, the fabric dancing upon her body, revealing the rhythmic rise-fall of her buttocks, the tremulous up-downing of her behind. But she was slowing down already. She no longer moved with the whirring blur of hummingbirds' wings, was no longer full of the brimming vitality of a Shango priestess. With Guy keeping her now, she had shoes and new dresses, and every Friday evening she went into the city to have her hair straightened. On Saturday nights she left with a bunch of girls who came into the Yard to meet her, with their careless laughter and insolent perfume, announcing their irritating, important emptiness and youth. They moved out of the Yard to the dance halls where they would spend the night dancing to Norman 'Tex', or Fitz-Vaughan Bryan, or Sel Duncan, returning early next morning, exchanging their stories and recounting the dance-hall fights, the rain of bottles and stones they had to dodge from, giggling at the terror of the night as if it had been a choice part of the evening's excitement.

Week nights she would slip across to Guy's place, boldly now, no longer the frightened deer approaching the hunter, boldly, with a kind of insolent challenge, daring anyone to condemn her. Now and again he saw Guy with her, the grabbing look in his eyes, talking in that inaudible whisper of conspiracy, acting as if they were strangers who had encountered each other by chance, as if their affair was a secret still to be guarded from everybody else.

Aldrick hurt for her, for the taming of her, the slowness and carelessness and the stupid vanity that was beginning to show in her. He felt helpless, watching her caught between Guy and her giggling friends and Miss Cleothilda, whose courting of her had resulted in such familiarity between them, that in the middle of the day you could hear Miss Cleothilda's voice cascading down her verandah, 'Sylvia! . . . Come let me show you something,' and Sylvia would turn from polishing her nails or putting her hair in curlers to go to her, her bottom up-downing, drop-rising in that slow, victorious drowsiness that was more and more becoming a part of her. In a little while you would hear their laughter, as if together they were savouring some sweet, conspiratorial pleasure that lifted them both above the Yard. It pained him, this wasting of Sylvia, this dulling of her; but he said nothing.

And he said nothing either, when he awoke one morning to the screams of Dolly, Pariag's wife, and rushed outside to see Dolly, her thin face bathed in tears, clasping and unclasping her hands, her mouth open and her jutting teeth below her lip in a frenzied screaming, and next to her, Pariag, standing quite still, his knees shaking and lips trembling, looking down at his Humber bicycle, lying crushed as by some monster, the two wheels bent, the chain off, the handle and fenders twisted, and the bell on

the ground – standing there before the cycle, saying
nothing, looking down at the bike, and everyone coming
out: Miss Olive and her children and Sylvia and Miss
Caroline from next door and Cleothilda, appearing on her
verandah in her nightgown and her morning face filled
with innocence, and Guy, looking down from his upstairs
room; and Dolly's screaming turning into sobs, and Pariag
saying nothing, just there standing, his lips and knees
trembling, and nobody venturing near, everybody keeping
back, holding back, as if they were at the edge of a fire or at
the rim of a volcano. Then Pariag, turning and seeing the
whole Yard around him, speaking in a voice that from its
fumbling, saddening softness rose to a crescendo of rage
and pain the more he spoke: 'You mash it up, eh! Ain't it
mash up! What you looking at now? What you looking at
the mash-up bike that you mash up for? Ain't you satisfied?' Asking a question that no one was expected to
answer. And as if seized by another rage, a taller rage, he
turned and began to advance upon Aldrick: 'You satisfy
now? You satisfy?' his voice softening with a new menace
(or was it appeal?) and was stopped only by his wife's
repeated screams: 'Boya! Boya! Oh, God, Boya!'

He allowed himself to be held by her and to be led by her
into the room they occupied, turning back, in his walking,
to look at his neighbours to say to them: 'It mash up. It
mash up. It mash up,' softly with the gentleness of a hurt
that went beyond the green Humber bicycle.

Pariag's bicycle lay on the ground for the remainder of the day. A bottle had been broken over it, and bits of paper and other trash, blowing across the Yard had got stuck in its fenders and between the spokes of its wheels. It lay there in the red dirt yard, not so much a wreck among bits of paper and broken glass, as a corpse laid out for viewing in the midst of wreaths, with the sense of life that is possessed by such corpses, made more living still by the people of the Yard who all day filed past it in a reverent silence, with that quality of fear and thoughtfulness with which the living view human death.

The next morning Pariag set it upon the one wheel that could still roll a little and, half lifting it, pushed it out of the Yard and into Alice Street, marching with it with that solemnity and bereavement and martyrdom reserved for wounded soldiers who, ambushed and outnumbered by their enemy, and, captive now, walk through the city occupied by their conquerors, with head held high and that attitude of undefeat that challenges the whole meaning of war – that asks the question: who, indeed, is victor, and who vanquished. He had no intention of making a report to the police. He walked the bike as if it were a wounded brother whom he was carrying in his arms through the very city, among the very people that had maimed him, so that the fellars at the Corner, hard, tough men like Fisheye, who since he came out of hospital had left Calvary Hill steelband and surrounded himself with a few young fellars, rebels all, recognized in him that calm, tall, dangerousness that was not even anger, was beyond it.

Aldrick was standing with them that afternoon, and he thought that he alone had seen it until he heard Fisheye say, 'Look at that fucking Indian!' Everybody grew silent. They watched Pariag carry-push the bicycle, and in that moment they felt themselves closer to him than they ever had. It was suddenly as if he had become alive, a person to them; and that moment, which was sacred, for it joined people together to a sense of their humanness and beauty, they would remember and recall long afterwards; so that one day when a fellar, seeing Pariag approach, and thinking him a target for their hustle, said: 'Hey! Let's touch that Indian for two bob,' Fisheye, without turning to look, would say, 'You know that Indian, boy?' and the young fellar who had recently come wild from the country, Sangre Grande, turned with respect and apology to Fisheye and said, 'I didn't know he was your friend. Sorry.' And Fisheye had leaned over and backhanded him across the lips, 'Get the fuck out of here, who say he is my friend?'

Pariag, too, felt the quality of their watching, felt touched that they had recognized him; and, for an instant he felt to drop the bicycle and rush towards them and embrace them, but he was in motion, and in the back of his mind was the fear that maybe he had felt wrong. Yet, it pained him that they had recognized him just at that moment when he was drawing away; and this pain brought a tallness to his walk, so that he was at that time both closer to them and farther from them. It would be across this distance and with this closeness that they would view each other henceforth, and it did not surprise Pariag at all that even a month after, when his bicycle had been repaired and he began again to carry on his business, Fisheye stopped demanding money from him.

In a way he missed it, for though it had been a relationship of predator and victim, he had felt that between himself and Fisheye there was a human bond. But he was

done with the Yard now. Finished with the Hill. When he
rode his bicycle through the streets now he didn't think of
himself as the Crazy Indian or anything; indeed, he seemed
to want to embrace now the very anonymity that he had
wanted to flee from earlier. He sold his barra and doubles,
gave people their change, said thank you and moved on. At
football games in the Savannah, he no longer cared to find
out who was winning. He was there to sell his goods and
make some money, and he did that. In the evening he rode
his bicycle carefully, and if a group of people walking home
from the football fell in step with him, he slowed down and
let them pass on. When he got home he washed himself,
ate his dinner, and decided with Dolly what they would
prepare for the morrow.

Before he bought the radio Dolly and he would play one
or two games of all fours and go to bed early, and he would
make love to Dolly, clasping her to him, and then,
wrenching free from the embrace, he would roll to one side
of the bed and to sleep, or sometimes he would lie on the
bed beside her, his hands joined under his head, his eyes
open in the darkness, and his thoughts far away; and he
would feel beside him, Dolly lying sleepless too, waiting
for him to say something. He thought about a lot of things
to say, but he didn't have the words to say them; and he
would feel her there beside him, thinking him asleep, so
still was he, reaching out a hand to touch him, tentatively,
half afraid, and he would endure the warm touch on his
body, trying in his mind to slip away from the touch,
without taking her hand off him. He would lie there
irritated not so much by her touch as that it was tentative
and half afraid; yet, he sensed he would hurt her if he took
her hand away, so he steeled himself, endured it, hoping
she'd drop off to sleep.

She didn't complain about anything. With all that had
happened, she never complained. She cooked his meals,
she cleaned, she boiled the split peas and kneaded the flour
and helped make the barra and doubles. He wondered what

things she thought about there alone in that room during the day. Did she think about life? Did she think about how all they were doing was just working? Did she think about how they were living in this city, just going on, invisible to the town, nobody knowing or caring if you dead or anything? In America he heard that a man could live his whole life in an apartment, in a room, and nobody know, and if he was dead nobody know, and if he was alive nobody know. And what was a man for? What was life for? He thought about those things. And then he would think about how patient and uncomplaining she was and how he didn't have the words to tell her things, and he would turn – and she, suddenly withdrawing her hand from touching him, afraid that it was she who was awakening him – and roll closer to her and reach out a hand and draw her to him, and would lie there embracing her until he fell asleep.

' You want to go and see an Indian picture?' he asked her one night, while they were lying in their separate sleep-lessness. And just like that she had turned and buried her face in his chest and cried.

'Hey! What happen to you? What happen?' But she didn't say anything, just went on crying silently, and then he realized that this was the first place he had asked her to go to, and he found that he had water in his eyes too. And he smoothened her hair and he didn't know what to say, and he held her close, and she held him, and he said: 'That is town for you!'

That same week they went to San Juan to see an Indian picture.

'You like it?' he asked when they came out.

She smiled, delighted, her teeth jutting out. She didn't even tell him that it was the first time she had been inside a cinema. But even so, the picture left them feeling very alone, for, for a moment it had plunged them into the fan-tastic and colourful world of India, bringing about in Pariag a longing for family, for home, for New Lands playground, playing all fours with Seenath, Ramjohn and Bali, for the smell of home, of saffron and green grass and cow dung steaming after a midday rain, and the sight of sugarcane, and the sound of keskidees and nanny-goats and the wind signalling an evening rain. So that walking up the Hill, he broke the silence: 'Let's go up to the country.'

And she said, 'Yes. . . . Yes.'

On Sunday morning they went by bus.

'Oh Lord, look Boya and Dolly!' his mother cried at sight of them. And he heard the echoes of the others, his family, gathered there in the yard around the steps, watching them come on: 'Look them! Look them! Look them!'

And before he fully settled in, he just had to go and see the playground again, go and see if Seenath, Bali and Ramjohn were still playing all fours, still singing bulls-eyes there. So he left Dolly and went up by the playground. But he didn't see anyone he knew. Not anyone. And he walked back to the house feeling funny, feeling alien.

Back at home, he was swept along by the bouts of greetings: his brothers, his cousins, his nieces and nephews, all of those who knew him, looking to see what town had added to him or taken from him, talking to him in that quality of falsetto family uses with visiting relatives, who have been abroad, who have been away, who come new as visitors, trying to capture the language the visitor had been living in:

'So you taking it easy? So Carnival was great in town?' trying to rope him into some game, or offering something to eat the way they would a stranger, creating, even in those gestures of appreciation and caring, a distance that Boya did not want between them, pushing him into a position of outsider even here.

And then he sat down with his father and two of his brothers, on the back steps of the house, not saying nothing, listening to his father talking, watching his father with those puzzled knots of veins on his forehead, strong still from his incessant labour, telling him that he only had two more instalments to pay on the house, telling about the goats he had bought and the galvanized iron sheets to build a shed, talking, chanting, about the cows and the grass and the nails and the cost of things, with that air of breathlessness as if he had come to accept the dealing with the mechanics of his surviving as an adventure.

'Well, tell me about Port of Spain,' his father said, after he had interrupted the mysteries of his surviving.

'It all right. It ain't no bed o' roses, but it all right,' he said, not wanting to talk but to flee, enduring the conversation as he would endure all the pleasant fuss of his relatives, finding consolation only in the small ones, his nieces and nephews, watching him, this uncle from town, trailing behind him wherever he moved as if they wanted to get a better view of him, as if they wanted to take a proper photograph of him in their minds before he disappeared back to Port of Spain. But, between them and him it was something that was beyond words, it was just a feeling: their knowing and his knowing that a bigger world stood outside the village, space to grow in, to spread in. He was glad to speak to them, no real big talk, just the ordinary: 'You going to school? What class you in?' They asked about football, and he talked to them a little about Malvern and Colts. He didn't like Maple. And all during his talking, his mother passing by, cutting in:

'You see Leela baby?'

'Which part of Port of Spain you-all really living?'

'You have water in the house . . . ?'

'. . . What about lights, Boya?'

Finally she sat down. 'Boya, your uncle tired ask for you.'

'What he ask for me for?'

'He is your uncle, boy, your family.'

His father sat down too. 'You must go and see your uncle. Already he saying is I who keeping you 'way from him.'

'Yes, Boya, go and see him; he tired ask for you.'

He went alone to see his uncle.

'You come to New Lands, you don't come to see me,' his uncle said, speaking in a soft, hoarse voice that he had kept well in control, guarded, the way he had guarded his increasing fortune, not giving not lending nor spending any more than was absolutely necessary. 'I send for you, you don't come. Family don't live so.' And he had looked at Pariag as if he was waiting now not so much for him to comment as to beg forgiveness and to proceed to ask the favour which he had already decided was the real purpose of his visit.

'I real busy in town, uncle.'

'You busy? . . . Take a little drink if you want to. I don't drink, you know,' he said, waving his hands to the sideboard and the liquor. 'You too busy for your family? You not drinking? Okay. Good. . . . They mash up your bicycle, and you ain't come and tell me nothing. Is so you want to live, among Creole people, like cat and dog, and forget your family. You have family, boy. Next thing you know, you leave your wife – who you didn't bring to see me. Why you didn't bring the girl to see me? Next thing you leave her in the house and they break in – they does break in people house in Port of Spain, you know. Why you want to stay down there for? And why you don't want to work for me? Your father work for me, and your brothers too. I don't rob them. I try to help my family.'

And, sitting there in the huge chair in the huge wooden room, with the bright curtains and the light coming through the louvres bringing a shadow of an avocado tree waving outside the window, Pariag thought of Port of Spain, of the Hill, of the people there, of his bicycle, of the efforts he had made to be friends with them, to be a person among people in a bigger world. He looked at his uncle, owning now a cinema in New Lands and a sawmill and trucks and a lumber yard and a whole settlement that he called Ramlogan Village. He was family, yes; but, a world was outside. He hadn't wanted to have to choose between them. But, in a way, he had made his choice already. He wanted to be a man, to join the world, be part of a bigger something in a bigger somewhere, to stretch out, extend himself, be a man among people.

'You not saying nothing,' his uncle said.

'Uncle, I don't know what to say. I . . . I trying for myself. Is not that I don't have thanks for you or anything . . . I trying for myself.'

And, returning to Port of Spain and his little room later that evening, he and Dolly and the gifts of ground provisions and hill rice that his parents had given him, he still felt alone.

'You shouldn'ta tell them,' he said to Dolly, 'about the bicycle. But is all right.'

In a way he hated going back to this Hill and these people, but his course had been set. He wasn't going to work for his uncle either.

Some nights later, he turned to Dolly on the bed.

'Maybe is not because I is Indian,' he said to Dolly. 'Maybe the Creole people just fuck-up.'

Many months later Pariag would be riding up Calvary Hill, and he would see Fisheye and Aldrick and some fellars from Alice Street corner crammed into a police jeep speeding into Port of Spain. He tried to dash out of their path, but the jeep slowed down, and Fisheye, a gun in his hand, had leaned over the window to wave at him and shout: 'Power to you, Brother!' It had moved him.

'Girl,' he said, telling Dolly about it later, 'these people not fuck-up. They crazy!'

The New Yard

By the time August came around, the Yard was a changed place. Miss Cleothilda had reasserted herself once more, not with quite the same careless pompousness of old, but with a new wisdom. Now she was a little less disrespectful to Miss Olive; Sylvia had become her friend, if not her protégée; and Philo, if gossip was to be believed, her man. At least he was now going openly beyond her verandah. This the Yard chose to view as their own personal victory. They saw it as the surrendering in Miss Cleothilda of a superiority that she could no longer claim, as a kind of coming down, a fall, that equalized all of them and that qualified her as a person in their eyes. Even Miss Caroline, her most persevering enemy, finally gave in and began to buy from her parlour. Though Miss Cleothilda continued to fuss with her customers as of old, Miss Caroline felt better able to bear it now.

As she explained to Olive: 'Now I could understand that she getting on so because is so she is and not because she feel she better than me. 'Cause I know now she can't feel she better; because she have a nigger man.'

Cleothilda neither denied nor confirmed the rumour. She moved about the Yard with a kind of bridal softness, fussing charitably about all her small concerns, attending the sick, listening with a frown and many sighs, and noddings to the confidence exposed to her, dispensing her advice in a softened motherly tone. She began to be called upon to be the adjudicator in matters of manners and taste, and as any of the Yard bought a new dress she would put it on and parade before Miss Cleothilda for her approval.

When Pariag's wife became pregnant she it was who led the line of women to the room in which the young couple lived, and made the greatest fuss over the girl.

'Look at us, Olive!' she said one day when the women were returning from attending to Dolly who was then having her first pains. 'All o' we is one. We have the same pains – Indian, Chinee, white, black, rich, poor. All o' we is one. All of us have to live here on this island.'

'And you know, we could live nice here,' she said wistfully. 'We could all live very nice here, if it wasn't for the one or two hooligans. Look at the weather how it nice! Look at the steelband boys how they gettin' civilize! You know, they don't fight again. They play their little music and go to work like anybody else. Is only the one or two hooligans that spoiling the place. They don't want to work, wouldn't pay their rent. They frightening people with their vexation. What they vex for? What they want to fight for? What they want, Miss Olive? You could tell me?'

But Miss Olive couldn't tell her.

'Miss Olive,' she said one day when only the two of them were in her parlour, 'you don't find our friend change?'

'Who?'

'Our friend,' she whispered, inclining her head in the direction of Aldrick's shack. 'Our dragon friend.'

'I find he quiet. But I can't really say how he change. He never do nothing before, except make his dragon costume. And I don't see him doing nothing more now. I really can't say how he change.'

'I tell you he change,' Cleothilda insisted. 'Long ago he used to make a joke, laugh, tease somebody. And it was kinda nice. He used to sleep and get up and stretch and yawn and we would know he alive. But now is a different kinda nothing. Now he serious and looking. Now he thinking and plotting. You think is crazy he going?'

'I don't know. Though they say when a lively fellar get serious so is to watch him.'

'I hear,' Cleothilda said, leaning over the counter to whisper, 'he not playing dragon next year.'

Miss Olive didn't say anything for a long while. She didn't say anything at all. Afterwards, when she was leaving, she took up her groceries as Miss Cleothilda recorded the cost in a book. She was very sad. 'He must be going crazy,' she said. 'He must be going crazy.'

Aldrick felt a change in himself. For a while it confused him. He thought about Sylvia a lot. But what really alarmed him was that the year was ending and he hadn't even thought about what dragon he would play in the coming Carnival.

He had tried to think of it, but his mind just wouldn't focus on Carnival. It scared him. Just the thought of not playing dragon made him feel naked and empty. In a way, he really didn't want to play dragon. It was as if he had outgrown it or something. But, what was he without the dragon? Who was he? What was there to define himself? What would he be able to point to and say: This is Aldrick? What?

Sitting there in the small confines of his little shack, surrounded by an aura of dragon costumes, of masquerade, was torture. He felt himself a stranger in that place; but he had to sleep somewhere, so he slept there. Now he began to find himself increasingly at the street corner in the company of Fisheye and some other fellows.

12   Outcasts

When Fisheye came out of hospital after Carnival, his chest in plaster and his ribs bandaged, he had headed straight for the Corner, his bulging eyes wise, a disdainful curl to his lips, putting his feet down on the ground in tall righteous limping steps as if, even with his injuries, he was alone the only man left on the Hill not traitor to his warriorhood, and had a duty now to uphold it, especially with the betrayal by Terry and Reds. So by the time Aldrick reached the Corner, no longer in tune with the Yard, dunned for rent by Guy, and helpless as Sylvia surrendered herself to Guy and Cleothilda, surrendering not only her own body and time of her own, but surrendering in herself that thing in herself that was not hers alone, that others – the whole Hill – could lay claim to; that spirit, that hope that had lived in the Yard, upheld in Miss Olive's patient resentment, Caroline's anger, and her own vitalness; that beauty of which she was custodian out of her innocence and daring and speed, that belief that there was ahead a better life, a nobler life, for which they, the whole Yard, were candidates out of their steadfast insistence on their right to a humanness unlinked to the possession of any goods or property, arrived at, realized, born to, in consequence of their being. So by the time Aldrick reached the Corner he would find Fisheye installed there, the head of a band of maybe six or seven young fellars, warriors, who still believed in their muscles, who hushed to their bosoms an anger older than themselves, their faces drawn into tight unhumorous grins, their gestures containing the slow sullen confidence and bravado of the old times, of days they didn't even seem to know were ending, now that Fuller Brothers had come in to sponsor the steelband, giving the fellows free jerseys and instruments free in exchange for 'good' behaviour.

So they were there now, the two of them, Fisheye and Aldrick, not yet drawn together in the same company; just there at the Corner, occupying the same territory, less a battlefield now than a haven, and more than a haven a vantage point, a podium from which they might view the Hill travelling up and down its main street. And they would be watching there, alert, wise, two captains, veterans of rebellion, Dragon and bad John, surrounded by six or seven young men, flagbearers of a disappearing warriorhood, who moved with such confidence that they would have been mistaken for the advance guard of an invincible army approaching from the bowels of hills and shanty towns. So that fellars, passing, turned and saluted them, calling out: 'Right-o Fisheye! Right-o Pistach! Right-o Adonis! Right-o Lloyd! Right-o!' And they would answer 'Right-o! Right-o! Right-o!' softly, deep from their bellies, from under their cap brims, each grand affirming sound swelling them up, making them believe in their potency.

Fisheye would nod his head, recognizing the salutes, retaining that judgemental distance, that power to condemn or applaud – a wave from him was treasured as a medallion of diamond – that was his not so much out of his personal strength and fearlessness, but that he alone could say: I have not surrendered.

It would be there at the Corner, watching the monotonous pedestrian journeying of people ensnared in their daily surviving, a ritual impelled not even by greed, set in motion by that most noble and obscene reason: the wife, the children, the belly, the back, the foot; the need to keep on keeping on; it was seeing fellars as guiltily bowing and grinning to Fisheye and his warriors, out of that need to touch that freedom that was once their own, that lived still, to join themselves to that hope that in themselves they had somehow abandoned; it would be there at the Corner that Aldrick realized that he did not have the courage to do it; that even though he knew that this pose of rebellion was not power, that to abandon it for that living paraded before him was a more profound treason, a surrender, a kind of death he had not yet achieved. And though he had no world to offer, no plan, no life that in itself gave the power to be a man, a person, he felt that he would like to try to save Sylvia — at least try to help her hold out a little longer, get a little older before she surrendered that beauty and life and spirit that was given her for herself to wear and become and proclaim. Even though he had no place to put her, no life to offer.

'Sylvia!' He tried to get her attention, to get her to stop and listen to him, to turn from the Friday night fêting and Cleothilda's gossiping and the talk of her giggling friends and the silly resentment she still bore him and look at herself. 'Girl, your life is yours. You don't have to spite me. Is your life.'

'I know is my life.'

'I mean, is your life for you to live. Is yours alone. You don't have to let vexation or revenge rule you. You don't have to prove nothing to me.'

'To you? Aldrick, what make you think I even think 'bout you?'

She was always in a hurry whenever she saw him, and he had to, as it were, fling the words after her; and she would fling back her answers, saucily, as she moved on, swept on, not even wanting to give him the satisfaction of being listened to. One day she stood up. They were in the Yard.

'Talk,' she said, impatient already, knees bent backwards, arms akimbo. 'I listening.' And before he could get a word out, she was sweeping off: 'You ask me to listen, I stand up. Why you don't talk? You know what! Aldrick, you don't have nothing to say.'

'You know what you want, Sylvia,' he said, his anger overpowering him, 'you want a good fuck.'

'Well, you is one man not going to give it to me.'

And he had felt a sadness, a caring. 'Girl,' he said, 'this is the kinda life you want for yourself? This kinda living? This shit?'

For once her face lost its confident carelessness, her eyes softened and her mouth trembled at the corners. 'You could give me something better?' And she had looked at him, into his eyes. 'Eh?' And he had no answer. So that Philo, coming into the Yard, seeing her strut off, could walk up to Aldrick, jingling the keys to his car in one hand and pushing up the brim of his white panama hat with the other, and say with that wisdom with which he now cruised through the world: 'You shoulda buy the costume for her, when you had the chance.'

'Yes, I shoulda really buy the costume for her,' Aldrick answered.

'Well, don't kill yourself. Let's go for a drink,' said Philo. 'I have my car here.'

Aldrick hesitated.

Since Philo started to become popular and got a regular job singing in a night club and bought the car and began to walk past Cleothilda's verandah into her house to, as the Yard asserted, her bed, it was as if life had revealed to him the full face of a humour that he seemed now to want to share with his old friends. Yet, though he made it his duty to seek out Aldrick to offer him a ride in his car, to take him for drinks at Zipless where all the girls knew him, and talk and drink and play juke box music, Aldrick didn't feel so comfortable with him any more.

Philo's success confused Aldrick. He was glad for him, and everything, but he didn't feel comfortable with him; and it was only out of fear of hurting Philo's feelings that he suffered himself to accept the invitation Philo gave and to be enraptured by the speed of Philo's car and the conquest of Philo's women and the quality of his scarves.

Aldrick felt it would be better if Philo moved on on his own, but Philo was bent on proving that he had not changed, that the friendship between the two of them was the same. Indeed, Philo began to express a new caring for the Hill and the fellars at the Corner. Some days he would pull up at the Corner and buy a bottle and break the seal with Fisheye and the fellars and sit down on the pavement and talk and laugh. Fisheye didn't like it. He didn't trust it, so much so that one day he moved to say to Aldrick: 'What that fellar trying?'

'How you mean?'

'I mean, he always so glad, so happy to be alive in this world, so . . . so laughing.'

'What wrong with that?'

'Nothing. Nothing . . . Is just that he so fucking happy all the time. Know what I mean?' He had turned to the fellars around him: 'Know what I mean?'

And the fellars had nodded in understanding.

Philo would have been in agony if he had heard that. Sometimes, sitting down with Aldrick, he would say, 'Man, we is the same fellars, you and me. Anywhere you see me, don't be afraid to call out to me. If I with the governor, call out to me. You and me is friend.'

To Aldrick, it seemed as if Philo's success had become almost a matter of apology. Philo decorated himself in gaudy shirts and broad-brimmed hats with long colourful feathers stuck in them, as if he wanted to hide himself, to make himself appear so cosquel that any fool would know that he had to be found elsewhere, apart from the costume, within it.

So now Philo was saying, a hurt look on his face, 'You don't feel to come and take a drink with me?'

'Okay,' Aldrick said, despite himself, 'let's go.'

So they went to Zipless, a place with low lights even in the day, and lots of waitresses. 'If you see one you like, just tell me,' Philo whispered, warm, buoyant again.

They all knew him and they came forward at his coming,

'Philo! Philo! Philo,' and he hugged them to him two at a time, then walked to his accustomed seat, two of the girls following him, and after taking his order, sitting at the table with them.

'I want to be with my people, man,' he said. 'I want my friends to be happy for me. I want fellars who know me when they look at me to say, There is Philo! There is Me! You know what I mean, Merle? Know what I mean, Rita?' And the girls smiled and nodded their heads.

They drank scotch, and Philo talked. 'I ain't change, Aldrick. I is the same man. I is still Calvary Hill, no matter what you see me do, you is me and I is you. I want my friends to understand me, man. I want you to understand me,' Philo said, leaning over and holding Aldrick by the shoulder, the whisky on his breath blowing into Aldrick's face. 'Years I struggle alone, man. I struggle. I belong to myself, man. Ain't you belong to yourself, Aldrick? And Merle, you? And Rita, you too? For years I struggle. Like a dog. People wouldn't let their daughter talk to me because I is a calypsonian. Alone, and now I get a break. I know it's a break, luck. I get a break. I want my friends around,' he said, hugging Aldrick with one hand and Rita with the other, then disengaging her to pinch Merle's face. 'What life for, man? What the struggle for if your friends leave you alone. If they don't understand you, man. This woman, Cleothilda, been in my blood for years. Listen Aldrick: this woman! Imagine me, a young calypsonian, twenty years old, and I see this woman, Cleothilda Alvarez, on stage in the Queen's Park Savannah with the pick of the Carnival queens, and though she didn't win, she nice. She nice, nice, nice. And I don't know why – if is stupid I stupid, or if is so the world is, I fall in love. Is not even love. Love ain't so wicked. I decide that I want this woman for my own; but, I can't even go near her. I don't know what to tell her when I see her. I can't talk. And she don't know if I living. And nothing I do I could get she out my mind. And then, one day, man. One day, Aldrick. One day,

I go and say, "Cleothilda, open the door," and she open it.
She open the door, man. You know what that is?'

'Your drink turning water,' Aldrick said.

'You know what that is, man?' Philo asked, gripping
Aldrick's shoulder, ignoring his drink. 'What I could do?
What you would do? Eh, man? You have to let the fellars
know the kinda man I is, Aldrick. I is we.'

'Okay,' Aldrick had said. 'Okay.'

But how could you explain such a thing to the Corner.
Fellars were warriors there. How could you even begin
such a talk?

'That fellar is your friend?' Fisheye asked Aldrick one day,
his voice soft, already challenging, in his tone, making a
clear separation between himself and Philo, to whom he
was alluding.

Philo had just come from up the Hill and was going
down slow, his head half way out the car, waving, calling
out to the fellars at the Corner in a loud voice, to each, indi-
vidually, by name, not only to let the girls in the car with
him know that he was known on the Hill, but to let the
fellars whom he called know that he embraced them; they
were friends of his. Aldrick had waved back to him, and
Philo had stopped the car, keeping the engine running, put
his head out the window, with his hat with the long red
feather in it, talking a little too loud over the baffling
engine, waving his hand with the thick gold ring on the
middle finger, doing his best to let the girls know and to let
the fellars know too that he was loved, and that he loved
them all. So that Fisheye, for all the discomfort he must
have felt at being part of this performance, was human
enough not to ignore him, waved, if a little curtly, and
stood leaning against the wall, a kind of detached watching
in his eyes, a tight smile on his lips, taking a good look at
Philo's performance, even while not wanting to bring him
down in front the girls, not wanting the girls to turn to him

and say: 'But I thought you said you have friends on the Hill.'

So it would be after Philo left, the vehicle going down the Hill slow, reluctantly, respectfully, as Philo might have left had he been on foot; it would be after Philo's departure, with the fellars still caught in the emotion of Philo's greeting and performance, quiet in a reflective silence that was almost breathtaking; that if someone were to speak he would have to take a deep breath, and even then, the sound that would come from him would not necessarily be words at all, but some kind of breathlessness. It would be in this silence that Fisheye would ask the question that was suddenly not so much a question as an accusation: 'That fellar is your friend?'

'He . . . he is everybody friend,' Aldrick had answered, hesitant, defensive.

'Well, he ain't my friend,' Fisheye said. 'That fellar just playing a game. He not one of us again. Cleothilda and Guy is his friend. He just come up here to fuck around, to show off, because he ain't have nobody else to show off his girls and his hat and his car to yet. Soon as he find his real clique, we wouldn't see him up here again.'

'Why you don't like the man?'

'Like him? I just don't want him on this Hill. Let him go and show off somewhere else,' Fisheye said. 'We don't live easy here. Life ain't no laughing with me. I is a warrior, a bad John. How he could be my friend?'

'He all right,' Aldrick said. 'He's a all right fellar.' But Aldrick said it weakly, without much conviction.

Indeed, Aldrick understood Fisheye's position. At the Corner, power lay not so much in the might of the small company as in their steadfast pose of rebellion, in their rejection of the ordinary world, its rewards and promises. How could Philo, with his flashy clothes and his car and his women, all gained in the service of that other world against which they were rebelling, be their friend? Yet, Philo was a friend. Maybe he did show off; but, it was more than that. Aldrick thought to try to explain it, to defend Philo as a friend should, but he didn't know how to explain it. He didn't know. And so he began even then to console himself with the thought that Philo had chosen his success, had, at least, called it forth, worked for it. If it were a burden now, Aldrick felt that Philo was the one to bear it for himself.

'I don't want him on this Hill,' Fisheye said.

Aldrick felt the fellars' eyes on him. Even they expected some sort of defence, some sort of resistance from him. This angered him; and on the heels of this anger came resentment against Philo for getting him into this position, and frustration with himself at not being able to say the words, to explain the situation to the fellars, indeed, to explain to himself. And it was less through his own conviction that Philo was a menace to the warriorhood at the Corner than his inability to hold the two ideas in his brain – Philo as a friend, and Philo as threat; Philo as play-boy, and Philo as a brother from the Hill – and let his action flow from that whole that he betrayed his friend.

Afterwards, he would recognize it as a more profound betrayal of himself. It was his insistence on retaining an innocence, on choosing the right path, that denied growth in himself, denied the truth of his own feelings. It was the feeling that he had to choose in a situation where there was no choice, really; in a situation where the best he could do was to trust himself and try to understand, and move on. Philo was maybe many things, but, Philo was still his friend.

And indeed, it wasn't as if he didn't know it. He felt it. He felt: this man is my friend. He felt it. But he felt other things too. And maybe it was easier to be rebel, to be warrior on the Corner, with Fisheye and the fellars with stern face and few words, watching the Hill people move in their insistent surviving, their little laughter, their brisk tread, their hesitant hellos. Maybe it was purer; but, it wasn't the truth.

But he didn't know that yet, that morning; and he

wouldn't learn it until afterwards, in prison. He would begin to trust himself, the different feelings in himself, the contradictions in himself.

On another day, Philo drove up the Hill. Two girls were crammed in the front seat with him. Philo, as usual, had waved, and Aldrick had waved back, thinking then to stop him and warn him of what reception lay in store for him at the Corner; but, to do so, he felt, would call forth an explanation; and he didn't know how to explain his own treachery to Philo. It wasn't enough, he felt, to say: 'Fisheye say he don't want you on the Hill.' So when Aldrick saw the car stop on its way down, as he had guessed it would, and saw Philo emerging from the front seat, he and his two girls, with a bottle of scotch in one hand, and the girls following him, laughing, all of them, Philo, having no reason to suspect what lay ahead of him, since apparently, nobody had told him anything, coming on jauntily, the feather bobbing in his hat, calling out the fellars by name, not even knowing yet that they were not answering, not realizing that with his scotch which he had come to drink with the fellars and his girls, he was putting Fisheye in a situation in which he could do nothing but refuse not only the scotch he had come to offer, but, in order to justify that refusal, reject him, his whole self and stance. When he (Aldrick) saw that, and himself leaning on the wall, not moving, he knew that he had chosen his side; and out of a concern for Philo whom he had curiously decided was no longer his friend, since he (Philo) could not carry out the posture and substance of their rebellion, he hoped that the blow Philo would receive would fall quickly and that the bonds that he (Aldrick) had already cut, would be cut quickly, knowing even then that it was sorta foolish.

'Fellars,' Philo said, touching his hat not so much straightening it as to see if it was still there, 'How life going?' realizing now for the first time that no answer had come back to him. 'I bring a bottle a scotch for us to hit.

Fish!' standing in front of Fisheye who would presently rock back on his heels and say: 'Philo, you ain't have no friend here. You is a big shot. It ain't have no big shot here,' his voice already steady and cold and with an edge of anger, renewing on his own an old provocation he felt.

'Fisheye, is me, man. Is me, Philo. Aldrick . . . Pistach . . . Adonis . . . fellars, I just stop by to say hello and take a drink with you. . . . Shit, man, what kinda joke this is. Come, let me open the scotch. Anybody have a glass,' turning the cap of the scotch and pouring out a little on the ground, saying, 'We can't forget the spirits of the dead,' holding out the bottle to Fisheye. 'You drink first. We ain't have no cup.'

And Fisheye saying: 'I tell you you ain't have no fuckin' friend here.' And when Philo kept his hand outstretched with the proffered bottle, as if it angered Fisheye, shamed him to a larger rage, his own hand darted out to flick aside the bottle – 'Take your fuckin' scotch and go from here' – following through to strike the face of the girl who stood at the side of Philo.

Philo understood then. Or maybe he still didn't understand, stood there watching the girl with her hands over her face crying, watching the scotch on the ground, watching around at the fellars into each of their faces, saying finally, softly: 'So you hit the girl, eh, Fisheye?'

Aldrick would move then. 'You better leave here, Philo,' he said. 'You better go.'

'But Aldrick, we is friends, man,' Philo was saying, still not understanding. And Aldrick, not touching him and not explaining, afraid to do that, 'You better go. Take the girl and go.'

'Aldrick, we is friends, you and me. And you know me.' Philo was insisting.

'I don't want you on this Corner,' Fisheye said, strengthening his voice to hide, obscure, whatever wrong he felt in himself.

'I born here, man,' Philo said. 'But why hit the girl?'

'Go, Philo. Take the girl and go.'

'Aldrick you didn't tell them that I is Calvary Hill, that I is one of them, that we is we.'

The other girl had reached the car, and she honked the horn impatiently. She was afraid. Philo looked to the car. He held the girl beside him by the hand, she had stopped crying.

'So is war between us, then, eh Fisheye,' Philo said softly.

'Is war,' Fisheye said.

'Okay,' Philo said softly, turned around and left, going very slowly, holding the girl by the hand, making short sad steps in his new black and white suede shoes. 'I going,' looking at Aldrick.

'The man is a enemy man,' Fisheye said. 'How he could be friend to me?'

'Is war!' Fisheye said to the silent men around him as Philo's car moved down the Hill; and not one of them suspected that there was any contest here. How could Philo fight them?

Aldrick was saddened by the entire episode; but, he thought that that was how the world went. Whenever in conversation he said, 'It's a fucked-up world,' he knew exactly what he was saying.

Carnival was approaching. Everybody was getting busy to prepare their costumes, but Aldrick, watching from his station at the Corner, just felt kinda odd in the whole Carnival. He just kinda felt odd. Every night he dreamt of Carnival dragons; but, in the day, he just kinda felt odd. No. He didn't think he was going to play Dragon for Carnival. Everywhere he went he found himself having to give explanations; but, he didn't even talk about it. Even the Yard seemed ready to forgive him. And, one month's end, Guy coming to his room on the pretext of coming to collect the rent money, was moved to ask with concern that he tried to mask with a tough tone: 'What happen? Where is your dragon costume?'

The Yard didn't know by what means he had arrived at his decision not to play masquerade, if decision it was. They thought that it needed some kind of heroism possessed by extraordinary men, some tremendous act of will, to refrain from playing masquerade; so they began to look at him with a new respect and puzzlement. They couldn't understand him. For his own part, Aldrick just watched on, spending his days at the Corner with Fisheye and the fellars, and his nights at the gambling club where, with Carnival in the air, men seemed to play cards less carefully.

He had clean forgotten Philo and his threat when one day, he heard Philo singing a calypso over the radio:

> *Hooligans in Port of Spain messing up the place*
> *Last night one of them slap my girl in she face*
> *The next time they see me, they better beware,*
> *I have an axe in my hand, a pistol in my waist,*
> *When my gun shoot off the police could make their case.*

> *Why they so jealous I really don't know*
> *I was their friend no so long ago*
> *Since I start to get fame they grinding their teeth*
> *They ready to eat me up like salmon meat*
> *The next time they see me they better come straight*
> *I have a dagger in my hand, a pistol in my waist,*
> *When I protect myself, the police could make their case.*

The calypso was an immediate hit. The radio stations took it up, the juke boxes played it, and, in the calypso tent, Philo received encore after encore when he sang it. It would be on the strength of that calypso that he would later be crowned Calypso King that Carnival.

Aldrick didn't understand it. What he did not know then was that Philo's attack on the Corner had come at a time when multitudes of people keenly felt the need to cut their

ties with the Corners in their own communities. These
were people who had inherited the rebellion bequeathed
them by their parents, upheld by bad Johns, Dragons,
Stickmen, bursting forth in the steelbands, crowning
warriors in Calvary Hill, Laventille, John John, Belmont,
St James, Morvant, but people for whom times had
changed. Something had happened. They had jobs now,
had responsibility now for the surviving of families, they
could no longer afford rebellion at the Corner. They felt
guilty turning away from it. Yet, they needed to move on.
They had to move on. But they could not move on with that
guilt. They could not move on, with the Corner still part of
them. They had to choose, they felt; and, it was because
they were unable to hold in their minds the two
contradictory ideas – their resistance and surviving, their
rebellion and their decency; because they felt that they had
to be one or the other in order to move on, they needed to
cut ties with the Corner. So it was that Philo's calypso
became a statement for them all. This would be the epitaph
to their rebellion.

Right after Carnival the police felt secure enough to launch
a campaign to rid the Corners of 'hooligans', and they came
into Calvary Hill now, no longer hesitant, respectful, but
prepared to stop their jeeps and harass and intimidate and
arrest at any show of resistance. Aldrick watched this
happening. The power of the Dragon even to threaten was
coming to an end; but he remained there at the Corner out
of a stubborn pride and loyalty, moving when the police
came and returning at their leaving, so that Fisheye would
watch him and say: 'You is man. All those fuckin' cowards
run; you stand up. You is man.'
    Out of Fisheye's trust and approval now, Aldrick was
promoted to a kind of lieutenant in the small guerrilla band
that was not so much guerrilla as the last remains of a
defeated army, that refused to surrender, indeed, to
acknowledge defeat, that would keep on fighting even after

hope for victory had ended, out of not knowing what else to
do.

'We is the last ones. The last fuckin' warriors. Look at
that!' Fisheye said, recalling the old days, the carnivals, the
warriors: Mastifay, Tom Keen, Batman, Baron. 'Look at
that!'

And they would remain there on the Corner, watching
the people flow down the Hill; and sometimes they would
laugh.

'Look at that man face,' a fellar would say of a man. 'He
going to work. Look at him!'

It was indeed funny to see the faces, the serious stupidity
of the faces, the important stupidity . . .

'And they don't own one damn thing . . . Hey! Gimme a
dollar!'

'I only have sixty cents.'

'Gimme!'

'You can't sorry for these people, Aldrick,' Fisheye said.
'They is traitors, every one of them. They only want a
excuse to be slaves again.'

But Aldrick wasn't so sure. He thought of Sylvia often.
She had wanted to move in with him in the little one room
shack. He had turned her down.

'Maybe it's their best they doing, man,' he said.

'Man,' Fisheye said, 'all of us come from this same hill.
All of us go through the same hell. How that could be
their best?'

'I don't know, man,' Aldrick said. 'I don't know.'

'You too soft. Softness will kill you.'

He watched the police jeeps move in, boldly now, as if
they knew that this band of men here at the Corner was not
even representative of the army, any army barracked on the
Hill, but a group of rebels fighting on out of stupidity or
ignorance, not even out of courage, for there was no battle
they could win.

'Move on! Move on! This is the last warning. Next time
you going straight in the van.'

And they would move on sullenly, muttering abuses under their breaths, regrouping after the sound of the jeep had died away, fixing themselves defiantly back in place, waiting for the other jeep to come, to go through the same process again.

'You see me,' Fisheye said one day, 'I going to kill a policeman.'

'You going to kill a police?' Aldrick asked.

'So help me God!' Fisheye said.

To Aldrick their problem went far beyond the police. It seemed to him that they were losing a battle with the times, with the people on the Hill. The people wanted to move on, to change, to make peace with their condition, to surrender that rebellion they had lived for generations; and they saw Fisheye, Aldrick, and the other fellars at the Corner, boxed increasingly into that rectangle of pavement and street at the side of the shop at the foot of the Hill as the witnesses to that bequeathal, who continued to fight on, whose eyes disturbed, challenged, accused them of abandoning their sacred war, that they (Fisheye and Aldrick and the fellars) continued to wage. So that these people began to view them, these rebels, not so much as the disturbing conscience they had become, but as the root cause of their problems.

'Is these fellars by the Corner that spoiling the place. They wouldn't work. They wouldn't die, just there with their eyes watching with fire . . .'

' . . . Waiting to rise one day and commit murder.'

To lend substance to their mutterings, they decided that they were afraid to venture out at night.

'Not me. I ain't walking by that Corner after dark.'

They warned their girl children, 'Walk straight. If they trouble you, call the police.'

And suddenly the Corner was bad again. Fisheye and Aldrick and the others had power, even with the harassment of the police. People were afraid of them. They were Dragons, bad Johns, thieves and rapists. Aldrick couldn't believe that these people, looking at them as enemies, were the ones he had lived seventeen years among.

'These people is beast,' Fisheye said. 'Play soft with them and they eat you alive.'

Aldrick began to join in the mocking and abuse with which Fisheye and the others retaliated, and, like Fisheye, he sought to terrorize them to show up their stupidity. But it was painful. These people – he had lived side by side with them for too long. What he really wanted was to show them their error, to make them see that they, Fisheye and Liberty and Adonis and Smalls, were of them, their own, and all this stupidness wasn't called for.

He watched Sylvia going up and down the Hill, her high heels clopping, her dress tail swinging, her arse walking across itself in rhythm with a steelband beating within her flesh, knowing by now that she nice, because her hair press and her dress new, and her fingernails polish with the same colour purple of her lipstick, and her face powder and her eyebrows is two lines across her forehead, and her handbag, swinging on her arm, have a few dollars in it. It hurt him to see her going by with her head in the air, with that haste, her face serious and eyes looking straight through people like they is not people. It hurt him to see her going by forcing that tall swing of her young limbs into that brisk mincing gait of one of those office ladies, or a nurse walking down the corridor of a ward she is in charge of, passing people like nobody ain't nutten unless you is the doctor. And fellars liked her. Fellars at the Corner liked the girl, half way understood her, for they had grown up with her and had touched her legs when they were young together, and the bigger fellars were still charmed by her beauty, by that rhythm and sweep of her, by the fact that she was the Hill, she was their own; and they would have fought for her. They would have lifted her up. They would have made her queen.

'Girl, don't do that to us,' he told her. 'You ain't Cleothilda. You is you, girl; and you young and you nice for your own self without anybody. You ain't them, and they can't make you and they ain't make you, not with their gifts or their friendship. Why you behaving like this for? We is you, girl. And if you have to friend with Guy because he could give you some cash, we ain't against you. Don't be ugly to us.'

'Leave me alone. I don't want no advice from you.'

'Girl, how I could leave you alone?' he asked her. 'Tell me! Tell me, how I could leave you alone?'

13   The Dragon Dance

No one knew where Fisheye got the pistol from. He appeared one morning, long after Aldrick and the others had assembled at the side of the shop at the Corner, clean-shaven, a pair of white buff shoes on, and black all over otherwise, except for the cigarette behind his ear; black pants, black belt, black silk jersey from his earlier days with Yvonne when he was one of the best dressed bad Johns in Port of Spain, and a black hat, the brim turned down right around, walking with that slow, tall, prancing crawl so that there was time enough for fellars to see him approaching and to say: 'Look, Fisheye coming!' and still have time to turn again and watch him, focus on him, walk towards them, calm, composed, filled with the potent silence of a blue cannon mounted on an open cart and dragged by two black horses whose only sound is the clopping on the roadway of their iron-shod hooves, and come to stand among them awkwardly, searching to invent gestures to accommodate the new persona he was projecting. He took the cigarette from behind his ear, asked for a light, and when he got it, drew in the smoke deeply, put a hand in his pocket and tugged out this thing, blowing out smoke in the same instant that he threw it (the thing) to Aldrick, so that Aldrick nearly dropped it. When he felt the cold metallic heaviness of it bounce against his palms, he grabbed it with his two hands and hugged it to his chest.

'Wh-Wha . . . t?' And he looked at Fisheye, catching him in that eye flash leaning against the wall of the shop building, one knee drawn up, the cigarette smoke drifting idly before his face that was already stretched into a long hard mischievous smile. 'Man, this is a gu-n!'

'Let them see it,' Fisheye said, not moving, when the others crowded around Aldrick. 'Touch it! Everybody, touch it! Look, I have the bullets.'

When it was returned to him, after it had been passed from hand to hand, the Chalice with the Body and Blood of Christ at Holy Communion, Fisheye, his voice a whisper, issued the command: 'Nobody leaving here 'til the police come. Today we ain't running.'

There were nine of them. The Calvary Hill Nine, the newspapers would soon be calling them – Fisheye; and Smalls; and Roper; and Adonis, a boy just out of juvenile prison, tall, calm, bone-tough, knock-kneed, with long hands and watching eyes from under a cap peak, waiting so desperately for an adventure he was ready to invent one; and Danny, a small jump fellar with an occasional stammer, who had chosen for himself the name Liberty Varlance, wearing as badges of his warriorhood a black whip around his waist and a white handled razor at his hip; and Synco-Utah Blane he called himself – Danny's friend, and lieutenant in a gang of youngsters Danny captained; and Crowley, a boy who was expelled from St Mary's College for hitting a priest with a bottle of red ink; and Pistach, a sharp witty fellow who was always talking about Fidel Castro, and was a kind of clown, seeing a joke in everything.

'I ready to dead this morning,' Fisheye said, speaking as if he was the last one, as if the others had made up their minds to die long before, and his decision was the last one required, and now that it was made, there was nothing more to be said; the action could begin.

Aldrick had himself made no preparation for his own dying; but Fisheye didn't even look at him.

'I want two fellars – you Crowley, and you Synco – to start a fight when you see the police coming,' Fisheye said. 'They will come and part the fight.' He chuckled, pulled his hat brim further over his eyes, and pushed his hands into his pockets.

'And when they part it?' Aldrick asked, after he had waited in vain for some query from one of the fellars.

'When they part it?' Fisheye said, savouring the question, while the others brought to bear upon Aldrick the full focus of their silence, not even turning their heads to look at him, and before Fisheye could complete his answer, Liberty Varlance was saying with his stammer, 'No-o-body ain't l-leaving here 'til the police come? Right?' and his riding pardner, Synco, was saying, 'Right!'

'When they part it,' Fisheye said, his voice tall, superior, nodding his head briskly, 'we will see.'

'Well, suppose they don't part it?' Aldrick persisted, knowing full well that in the eyes of the fellars he was already a traitor, but prepared to bear that to win the details of the plan of action.

'Something will happen,' Fisheye answered. And, with a dismissing disdain, he added, 'You frighten?'

Aldrick didn't say anything more then; but he would have a long time in prison to go over those words 'Something will happen' and come to understand that at that time there could have been no other answer, no more elaborate plan, for these men shared a belief that victory was won out of the justice of their cause and the courage of their soldiers. Plan? They needed no plan. To require a plan was to question the very truth of their cause and the bravery of their soldiers. Something, a miracle, would happen.

When the police jeep came to make its rounds, Crowley and Synco were on the pavement fighting. The jeep slowed down, but did not stop, the policemen pretending not to see what was happening.

'Hey! You don't see two people fighting?' Pistach called out.

'Why you don't stop them?' the policeman said. And as the jeep picked up speed, a moving truck laden with

furniture and beds, filling up the entire street appeared
from up the Hill, so that the police jeep had to stop. When
the truck reached almost upon the jeep, it stopped for the
jeep to back up for it to pass. The jeep backed up and waited
for the truck to proceed. The truck did not proceed. The
truck driver came outside waving a spanner and a screw-
driver in his hands and opened up the bonnet of the truck.
The two fighters had in the meantime taken their battle
into the street, right in front of the idling police jeep.

'Hey!' one of the policmen said, opening the door
hastily, angry at the entire situation, the stalled truck and
the insolence of the fighters in the street, so that though he
had a gun holstered at his hip, he didn't even think to take
it out. The other policeman squeezed out through the same
door since the jeep was right up against a concrete wall that
ran lengthwise down just that portion of the street. The
two of them proceeded to the fight which was not what they
wanted to do, they really wanted to go and see what the hell
was wrong with the truck, maybe charge the truck driver
with having a defective vehicle or something, but the fight
was right in front of them.

'Listen!' said one of the policemen, as the other
unlocked the back portion of the jeep where they put
prisoners, 'the two of you coming with me,' not drawing
his gun yet as the two combatants wrestled before him.
'Get up!'

The two men got up.

'Come, let's go to the station.' And the other policeman,
the one who had opened the door to the back of the jeep,
came over not so much to lend a hand as much as to add his
physical presence, the power of his uniform, to the
situation.

'Move!' the policeman said, only now putting his hand
on the gun buttoned down in a holster at his hip. 'Move
on!'

That was when Fisheye said the words that he would
recall to his death: 'Nobody ain't moving on,' and when the

policeman turned to the voice, they would see him standing beside the jeep and a little behind them, his hat brim pushed up from his eyes, his legs spread apart, slightly bow-legged, leaning back a little, with a pistol in his hand, a cowboy in a Western movie, braced against one of those storms of dust that always seem to sweep across the street, rolling hoops of brambles, just at the moment of the showdown between two nerveless rival gunmen. 'And take your hand off your holster.'

Fisheye might have remained frozen in his pose waiting for a challenge from the police, if Crowley hadn't said, 'Put up your hands and walk slow inside the van.' Then Fisheye moved, herding the policemen before him into the back of the open jeep. He followed them, then others of the nine piled in.

Smalls got into the driver's seat.

'Drive!' Fisheye said.

The jeep moved off.

They handcuffed the policemen to the side of the jeep, and took away their revolvers.

'Who here have the guts to kill a police?' Fisheye asked.

'I!' replied Liberty Varlance.

'Take this gun. Shoot if they try anything.'

'Where we going?' Smalls asked, driving.

'To the Square.' The answer came back as if it had been there just to be plucked out of the air.

Woodford Square is the centre of down-town Port of Spain, a few blocks away from the headquarters of the Trinidad Police Force. It was where politicians gave their speeches, and where, every day, groups of men would be assembled discussing politics and religion. Aldrick didn't bother to ask why they were going to the Square. He knew by then that this was his day to die. He had visions of policemen in riot helmets with sub machine guns barricading the street. He remembered his father and how he had died with his hands in his pockets, and he pushed his own hands into his pockets; but he soon pulled them out: everybody had to die for himself. He looked across at Fisheye leaning forward in the front seat as if now that he had come out to die in his black suit, bullets couldn't harm him. The others seemed too filled with their adventure to make dying a concern. The day belonged to them, had been there waiting for them, bequeathed to them years before, to fill it with their gestures. So that when Smalls, driving at breakneck speed down Frederick Street, looking from his rear view mirror, cried out almost with glee, 'Police behind us!' Fisheye, without any panic at all, in a kind of vital signalling of his power, leaned over the window and shot two bullets into the air, and Pistach, who had been fiddling with the megaphone all along the drive, now put it to his lips and began his astonishing announcement: 'This is the People's Liberation Army. We are armed and dangerous. We have two policemen prisoners. Any attempt to stop us will result in their death.'

Afterwards, in jail, he had asked Pistach what made him think to say that. Pistach said that he knew that that would frighten the authorities.

'They still behind?' Fisheye asked Smalls.

'They still there, yes.'

And Fisheye leaned over the window and shot another bullet into the air, as Pistach continued his warning: 'We are heavily armed. Do not take leave of your senses and try to attack us, for we shall kill your comrades . . . This is the People's Liberation Army demanding Freedom, Liberation and Justice . . . We are armed and dangerous . . .'

'They still behind?' Fisheye asked gleefully.

'Ha ha ha!'

'No. The bitches gone.'

The fellars in the jeep gave a cheer that Aldrick, to his surprise, felt himself vociferously joining.

Aldrick did not know what had come over him. There was suddenly a feeling of excitement, of power. He felt that they were soldiers in truth, warriors, an army, and he saw

before him again, his mother rocking the baby and his
father coming up the street striding, his hands scissoring
in front of him, and he saw Sylvia; and there was
something he wanted to say, something he wanted to
shout. So that when Pistach, his voice hoarse, cast his eyes
around the jeep for someone to relieve him of the
megaphone, Aldrick took it. And then he heard his own
voice saying, shouting, crying: 'This is the People's
Liberation Army, Shanty Town, Hill, Slum Army with
guns and jeep coming into the city seeking power, making
a cry for our people to rise, to rise up and take theyself
over; take over Laventille, Calvary Hill, Belmont, take over
John John, St James, Morvant, take power and rise to be
people for our own self, take power, take Pow-er, Pow-er!
Pow-er!'

When Aldrick came to himself, he was hoarse, and perspiration was streaming down his face. He handed the
megaphone back to Pistach and he didn't even know that
they had been circling Woodford Square for the last hour
until he heard the roar of the applauding crowd gathered in
the Square: 'Pow-er! Pow-er! Pow-er! Pow-er! Pow-er!'

And then he felt his whole body glow with a roasting
heat and a cold flash move across his stomach, through his
insides. People were shouting, crying out. They were
looking to them in the jeep, expecting something.

'We have them!' Fisheye cried, and he leaned over the
window and shot a bullet into the air.

'Wheee!' Adonis cried out. He was at the back of the jeep
with Liberty Varlance and the two policemen. 'Look at
police!'

When Aldrick looked back he saw hundreds of policemen
with rifles and riot helmets wheeling across the street just
in front of the Anglican cathedral.

'What we going to do now?' Liberty Varlance asked.

'Drive!' Fisheye said. And, to Pistach 'Gimme that
thing!'

Pistach handed over the megaphone.

'This is General Fisheye of the People's Liberation Army. We ain't making fun. We have two police here. If you attack us we will shoot them.' He handed the megaphone back to Pistach. 'You, tell them for me.'

'This is the People's Liberation Army . . .' Pistach began.

The jeep passed unhindered along the street.

'What we going to do now?' Aldrick asked.

'How you mean, what we going to do? Ain't we get past the police?'

'Yes, but what we going to do?'

'I don't understand you,' Fisheye said.

'I mean,' Aldrick asked, 'we going to just keep driving around until the police stop us?'

'I hungry,' Roper said. 'How we going to eat with the police following behind us everywhere we go?'

'They following?' Fisheye asked.

'Look behind; three of their jeeps,' Smalls said. 'And we can't drive too far without gasolene.'

'You frighten?' Fisheye asked.

'Who? Me?' protested Smalls.

Aldrick sat back as the jeep headed away from the city in the direction of Calvary Hill, going briskly through the curiously empty street. The others were looking back at the police following. He looked outside at the people as they gazed, listening to Pistach sounding the warning: 'We are the People's Liberation Army. This is our country. We demand it today. Today we are calling our people to come out, to rise up and take power! Rise and reclaim your manhood, people! Rise up!'

'This is action, eh,' Fisheye said to Aldrick. He was in his glee.

'You know we can't leave this jeep,' Aldrick said.

'You frighten?' Fisheye asked him.

'Yes,' Aldrick said. But he wasn't really frightened.

'They can't come out either,' Fisheye said, pointing at the police jeeps.

Why did the police not try to stop them that evening? This would be the question, plaguing Aldrick then, that the young lawyer the Nine had got to defend them, would ask again and again as the trial continued. Why did they sit back and allow them to enter the city, disturb the peace, exhort the population to rebellion, and then leave? Was it because they knew that cooped up in the jeep, without food or water or gasolene they would need to make a move to leave the jeep, and when they did they would attack them? Or were the authorities scared off by the warnings the Nine gave frantically all day and night? At least, why did they not cordon off the Calvary Hill area where the Nine spent the night inside the jeep? Why did they allow them to rest, to plan? Or, did they have some larger purpose? Why?

The next day was Tuesday. Aldrick had remained wide awake during the night, without a thought of sleep. He felt the calm power of a man surrounded by miracles, and he was very polite to the two captive policemen. As the jeep cruised slowly down the street – they would be going again to Woodford Square today – he had a feeling of being imprisoned in a dragon costume on Carnival Tuesday. This feeling pierced him more as he saw their route lined with people, no policemen in sight and, except for a few bicycles, no vehicles. It was as if they had been given a holiday and the keys to the city; and in a little while would come the roar of motor-cycles, and the limousine bearing the governor and his party would appear to join them. He didn't know then that exits to the city were closed and guarded and vehicles confined to certain streets.

Then he saw Sylvia in the crowd, not that he could miss her. She was wearing a red dress cut low at the bosom, and she was standing in the front on the edge of the pavement, with her hands folded into each other, and her mouth half open in wonder, the way a child might gape at his own brother or sister who appears costumed on the streets for Carnival, looking at him or her, trying to fit the two together. He thought to wave at her; but his hands did not

move. He couldn't be sure whether it was the presence of
the crowd that cowed him, or if he believed she would not
respond, would think it a vulgar show-off gesture from
him because there, with all eyes upon him, he could afford
to wave. Indeed, he felt it was the seriousness of the
occasion. He was already holding himself in that important
calm of the masquerader who parades before the judges,
filled with the sense of the character he portrays. A dragon
doesn't wave at a friend. So they slid away from each other,
their eyes locked that whole journey, hers asking: 'What?
What you doing there?' His seeking to say, 'I love you, but
you cannot understand.'

All the way to down-town stood lines of people in the
early morning. Older women with hats on or with towels
thrown around their shoulders against the dew, old men,
rake thin and grey, their eyes holding surprise and smiles
that made them look funny and young and wise; young
men, arms folded across their chests, their heads turned
slightly to one side, their faces with that look somewhere
between sullenness and nonchalance, as if they wanted to
be part of it and divorced from it, so that if the police asked
they could say: 'We know nothing of those fellars.' But
now and then one of them lifted his eyelids, and Aldrick
saw in that eye flash a flash that told of muscles rippling
under buttoned down sleeves. They will rise, he thought.
They will rise up! People will rise up if they see a light
. . . if they see a light.

Aldrick felt dangerous, like a wanted man. And he
wished that he had shouted 'I love you' to Sylvia for he
knew that today he was going to die.

He took the megaphone from Fisheye. He thought of his
father with his hands in his pockets at his death, and he
thought of his grandfather who had stuck with the promise
of the land for all those years, all those years, waiting, and
of the going, the leaving of his aunts and grandmother, and
the Hill, and his brothers and sisters whom he had not
seen for months, for years, all scattered, each one surviving

alone, screaming alone, dreaming alone; and he thought of
Basil, the boy, and of the children making dragon
costumes, indoctrinated at an early age to be the dragon, to
threaten and bluster, and of Sylvia and Miss Olive and
Caroline and of the little room that he did not own, did not
pay rent for.

'I want to go outside,' he said to Fisheye.

'You crazy?'

'I want to go outside. Stop the jeep.'

And Fisheye saw that he was serious; and he, Fisheye,
grew calm.

'I will stop the jeep, but you can't go outside.'

They were some distance away from Woodford Square
when the jeep stopped. The people following them
stopped too.

'Make no peace with slavery,' Aldrick cried. 'Make no
peace, for you have survived. You are here filling up the
shanty towns, prisons, slums, street corners, mental
asylums, brothels, hospitals. Make no peace with shanty
towns, dog shit, piss. We have to live as people, people.
We have to rise. Rise up. But how do you rise up when your
brothers are making peace for a few dollars? When sisters
selling their souls, and mothers and fathers selling their
children. How can you rise with rent to pay and children to
school, and watch hunger march across your yard and camp
inside your house? How can you not make peace?'

Aldrick said a phrase of which he would be very proud
long afterwards: 'I don't know.' But he hadn't expected
those words to come from him. He had wanted to stir them
up, to help, to make people know, to strengthen them. He
felt very disappointed at himself.

The jeep moved on to Woodford Square. There was not a
policeman in sight.

'You see any?' Smalls asked, looking back from his
driving.

'Not one,' Liberty Varlance said.

'I tell you, this is our country, we must take it,' Pistach

cried to the crowd gathered to hear them. 'We must cease to be slaves . . .'

Pistach talked, Fisheye talked, Aldrick talked, Adonis made his first effort that day before an applauding crowd that stood there waiting for something else, some kind of redemption, some saving.

'I hungry,' Roper said.

'Where the police?' Adonis wanted to know.

Aldrick, feeling an increasing impotence as they talked on, talked words that stirred the feelings but did little else, began to hope that the police would try to stop them. That would save them. But, they were not to be rescued by the police.

14   Prison Dance

'I will tell you why they did not stop them, Your Lordship, Ladies and Gentlemen of the jury . . .' said the young lawyer, standing tall, confident, inclining his face to first the judge and then the jury. Aldrick, sitting in the dock with Fisheye and the others, felt the court grow quiet so that it could hear the last sniffle from Crowley's mother, a tough stringy black woman with veins standing out on her hands, who, dressed in black, had sat listening to the Prosecutor outline all the horrible things of which her son had been accused, on the edge of her seat, crying into a white handkerchief. He watched the judge, his wig around his head like the large drooping ears of a Saint Bernard dog, hunched over his desk, keen, alert, with that implacable frown – the presiding umpire at the Queen's Park Oval in a cricket test-match between the West Indies and England, knowing that he was a black man and that he was there to interpret the law; and he would show them that he knew the law, so that if there was one thing they could say about any black West Indian judges, it would be that they knew the law; and this young chap, shuffling like a fast bowler at the start of his run up, would need to marshal his arguments well, for he was there to uphold the law, not to judge society nor to change men, but to do one civilized thing: uphold the Law; and neither his own blackness nor the fact that the woman with veined hands crying into a white handkerchief reminded him of his own mother, who died while he was studying in England, would have the slightest effect upon him. The Law had no friend, and at times, it had to disown even its one sister, Justice.

'I will tell you,' said the young lawyer, righteously.

He was thirty-four years old. When he was nine, he won a college exhibition from San Juan Government School and entered QRC – Queen's Royal College – the premier secondary school in the country; there he won a scholarship, placing third in the Cambridge examinations in the entire island, and went on to Oxford where he studied Law; and now he was back home, back home after having been through these elite schools; but he had not forgotten poverty, not that he ever knew it as a boy, since, from childhood in the house of his parents, the best of everything was reserved for him – the egg, the orange, the bottle of phospherine to give him an edge, to strengthen his brains; for he was the bright one, the one to push, the one to save; no, he had not forgotten poverty. And after his day's work he would put aside the ridiculous colonial wig and gown and saunter down the streets of San Juan in tennis shoes and go across to the Savannah and play a game of football with the boys, and afterwards go and have an ole talk with fellars who remembered him from schooldays, from San Juan Government School, fellars marvelling that he, one of them, their own, had been so far away, Oxford, England, and could still have that appreciation to come and sit down and take a drink in the back of Baby Joe shop with them. Fellars said he was a radical. They said he was a brain. But, for all his apparent casualness, he had read Marx and grounded on Fanon and Malcolm X and he was on the outskirts of what called itself a Socialist Movement, involving progressive professionals and fellows from the University of the West Indies.

No one was more suited to defend the Nine. He was tall, slim, black, good looking in a regular sort of way, with that imperious elegance about him so that he looked like a young prince who walked ordinary through the world so that he could be among his people without impediment of rank; but his gestures betrayed him: his walk, the modulation of his voice. Now he stood ramrod straight.

'They did not seek to stop them, because they knew that they would stop themselves; that they, frustrated as they were, were already outmanoeuvred, not by the police, nor by the closing of gas stations on their route, nor by the blocking of exits to the city, nor even by their thirst and hunger. They knew – the authorities knew – that Fisheye – Belasco John – would shoot bullets into the air, but that he wouldn't shoot anyone. They knew that Pistach would hurl tirades against the state, but that he wouldn't harm anyone. We have testimony to the effect that the young man who calls himself Liberty Varlance did say he had the guts to kill a policeman, but we do know that no policeman is dead.

'The authorities trusted these men to fail, that is why they made no move to stop them. They trusted that they would be unable to make of their frustration anything better than a dragon dance, a threatening gesture; that is why they did not attempt to stop them.

'. . . and if this is so, if it is that the authorities did anticipate, did forecast so accurately that these men would go no further than they did, would not harm anybody, then, how can we be trying them here today?

'The action undertaken by these men was an attempt to not even seize power, as we have seen, but to affirm a personhood for themselves, and beyond themselves, to proclaim a personhood for people deprived and illegitimized as they: the people of the Hill, of the slums and shanty towns.

'They came, as we have seen, without any plan or practice for what they might have attempted, desperately, spontaneously, trying to call forth by some magic a deliverance, asking for something to happen, looking for something to happen, not by plan but by the same magic that people who are oppressed reach for, that Moses reached for when he waved his staff and commanded the

Red Sea to part so that his people might flee the bondage of Pharaoh.

'Our country is young, our colonial inheritance is stifling,' said the young lawyer, tugging at the neck of his gown. 'When our people rise up to demand to decide for themselves that they should live, that they should be, it is no solution to jail them. Clearly, Your Lordship, Ladies and Gentlemen of the jury, someone else has been deciding how these people should live, someone else not living where they are living, someone else not living their lives; for if these people had been deciding for themselves how they should live, do you believe they would choose such streets in which to live, such houses to shelter them, such conditions? Do you believe they would choose street corners for their sons and prostitution for their daughters and hungry bellies for their infant children? Can we say yes? Can we say that human beings would so decide against themselves? If we say that, then we deny them humanity; we deny ourselves that faith in the brotherhood of man. We suggest the existence of better races, better people.

'Then, how hollow now sound our railings against slavery and colonialism.

'Rather than jail these men, we should applaud their courage to stand up to show us that injustices exist in our midst, that frustration and anger live among our people, that we should have the courage to attempt to lessen, if not eradicate.'

'That young fellar talk good, eh?' Fisheye said to Aldrick during a recess. 'Real good, eh?'

'Yes,' Aldrick said. 'He beg for us well.'

'You think they going to jail us after he talk so?'

'You expect them to let us go? Even if they believe what the lawyer tell them, you really expect they will let us go?'

'But, he say we didn't do nutten,' Pistach said. 'He say is frustration and anger. We is frustration and anger. You didn't hear him?'

'I is more than that, man,' Aldrick said. 'I was serious. I wanted us to take over the town, the island. I was serious.'

'You wanto know why the police really didn't stop us?' Aldrick said. They were riding in a van back to Golden Grove Prison. They had received their sentences: Aldrick six years, Fisheye seven, and the rest of the fellars between four and five. Adonis, the youngest, was not sentenced yet. He would go to the juvenile prison.

'The lawyer explain it already,' Pistach said.

'Is more than that. Is not only that they knew we couldn't win. They knew that. They guessed that. They knew we was just some fellars with guns who jump off the Corner and drive into town and shout liberation. They wanted to destroy us in our own eyes. They wanted to kill rebellion in us, to show us that even with no police to stop us we couldn't do nutten.'

'If we had a plan,' Roper said, 'things woulda be different. Then they woulda see action.'

'They knew we didn't have no plan. But more than that, they wanted us to realize that we can't win unless we beat them.'

'Well, yes,' Pistach said, 'how else we could win if we don't beat them?'

'They want to tell us that we can't be free unless we beat them, that we can't be men unless we win, that we don't have no claim to anything because we lose to them. You see, they want us to make winning a condition for freedom. I mean they want to make it appear that because we didn't have no plan, and because we didn't win that we don't have no right to be free, that we don't have no right to be people. So now that we lose this battle they intend for us to surrender, give up the right to be people. As if your right to be people and your strength to win is the same thing.'

'Is not the same thing?' Pistach asked. 'Is not the same thing? If you don't have power, how you going to be free?'

'People is people,' Roper said.

'They allow us to run loose until we give we self up so

that we could see for weself that all we could do is a dragon dance; all we could do is to threaten power, to show off power we have but don't know how to organize, how to use.'

Indeed, their efforts at rebellion was just a dragon dance. In jail the first thing Fisheye said with a kinda pride, kinda justifying to himself the seven years' sentence, was: 'I can't say they jail me for nutten; we play a mas', eh? We really play a mas'. We really had them frighten. We had them wondering if we was going to shoot down the town or what. We really play a mas', eh, Aldrick? You couldn't play a better dragon.'

'Yes, we played a mas',' Aldrick said. 'We played a dragon.'

And it was many months later, by which time Aldrick had grown accustomed to being in prison, to the food, the guards, his own silence, and he could see in perspective those two days without the regrets, the disappointment, the feeling of waste. They were sitting together – he, Fisheye, Smalls, Pistach and Roper.

'You know, we coulda play more than a mas',' he said.

'We coulda do what?' It seemed to surprise Fisheye, the idea. He was silent for a while. 'No, we couldn'ta do anything more. Everybody was too hungry. Two days we didn't eat.'

'We coulda do more than play a mas',' Aldrick said.

'You mean in the church? You mean, after we leave the Square we coulda start shooting? Or, you mean when we went to the cathedral we coulda stay right there, after we drink the wine and eat the communion bread?'

'Man, that woulda be twenty years,' Pistach said. 'They don't make joke with the Catholic church – Hey! Smalls could really drive, you know. All the police trailing us, and everybody hungry, and we don't know where to go, and sudden so, I just feel the jeep lean, and the engine bawl, and we clean through the cathedral gate and almost inside the church. That was real sweet driving, eh?'

'You mean,' Fisheye asked, 'we coulda hold those people we find praying in the cathedral? Hold them and tell the police if they try to come in we will shoot the people? That went through my mind. But, after those two women faint and all of them start to scream, I figger it going to be real hell to hold those people there . . . you mean, we shoulda stay in the cathedral? Nah! You can't mean that . . . is that what you mean?'

'That woulda be r-revolution,' Liberty Varlance said. 'They coulda t-try you for t-treason and put you before a f-firing squad for that.'

'What we was thinking? What was in our head?' Aldrick said.

'The way I was thinking was: this church is a tomb. All those police outside waiting, all these people inside bawling. You know those police coulda wait outside whole year. They coulda starve us in there,' Fisheye said.

'And all them saints and statues looking at me,' Pistach said. 'I nearly start to pray.'

'Lemme see! What was in my head? What you mean, what was in my head?' Fisheye said.

'Who had the guns?' Aldrick asked.

'Well, I had one, and Liberty still had the one that I give him to keep the police quiet. And after we jump out the jeep and leave the police handcuff to the jeep, he still had it . . . You mean, he shoulda shoot one o' the police?'

'I mean, we couldn't do what we didn't see to do. We couldn'ta enter where we had no vision to go.'

'Aldrick, man, I don't understand your talk,' Fisheye said. 'Since you in prison like you get holy or gone crazy or something. I don't understand that kinda talk.'

And then another day, months later, Fisheye came upon him in the prison library.

'I know what you mean. You mean,' Fisheye said, softly whispering as if he was revealing the plans to a conspiracy. 'You mean we didn't know what we was doing, not so? You mean, we was just nine crazy fellars with two guns and a police jeep, who wanted to attract attention. Ain't that what you mean?'

'Yes, we wanted to attract attention,' Aldrick said, closing the book he had been reading. 'So many things we coulda do, and all we wanted was to attract attention! How come everything we do we have to be appealing to somebody else? Always somebody to tell us if this right or wrong, if it good or bad. You ever notice that?'

'The steelband. Nobody didn't have to tell us nothing about the steelband.'

'They didn't bring adjudicators from England to judge the steelband competitions?'

'You mean, we don't *do* nutten?'

'Even with guns in we hand, even with power, we was looking to somebody else to make a decision. . . . Even when we have power, when we have guns. Is like we ain't have no self. I mean, we have a self but the self we have is for somebody else. Is like even when we acting we ain't the actor. Know what I mean? Eh?'

'I can't see how myself is for somebody else.'

'You have to see that,' Aldrick said, 'to see how we coulda do more than play a mas'.'

'Okay,' Fisheye said, backing out of the library, 'but watch those books they don't send you crazy, man.'

Then about two weeks later Aldrick was in the ping-pong room waiting for a game. Pistach was there and Liberty Varlance was on the board. They were playing knock out games, and nobody could beat Varlance off the board. Fisheye came and sat down next to Aldrick. He watched the games, and he didn't say nothing. Then, it burst out of him: 'You mean, I stick up the police, and we capture the jeep and parade the town, and it wasn't for myself, for me? That is what you saying?'

'Yes. We was speaking to them, shouting to them. We was saying to them, "Look at us! We is people!" We wasn't ready to take over nothing for we own self. We put the

responsibility on them to act, to do something. You don't
see that? The way children cry, so their parents will pick
them up. You don't see that?'

'But,' Pistach said, 'they responsible. They is the
authorities.'

'We is people. I, you, you, for we own self. For you and
for you and for your own self. We is people with the
responsibility for we own self. And as long as we appeal to
others, to the authorities, they will do what they want. We
have to act for we.'

'Man, you beat me,' Fisheye said, looking at him with
new respect, distance between them suddenly that neither
of them would try to bridge in a hurry; so that from that day
Fisheye didn't seek him out, and the others passed him,
respectful and half-fearing, saying to themselves singly
what together they had agreed: 'This man crazy!'

So that the five years and two months he spent in prison
were spent mostly alone, reading the books he could lay
hands on, exercising, playing games silently, minding his
business, in a kind of web, a kind of cloud, a stranger in a
country where he knew no one, was barred from others by a
difference in language, where there was no one to share the
sights with, no one to whom to say, 'Hey, that's a pretty
girl!' or, 'Look at that flower!' or 'Hear that melody!' or to
tell the thoughts from his head. And then one day he was
strong enough, he felt, to approach them in the ping-pong
room where they congregated playing knock out ping-pong
games. He was strong enough then to walk up to Fisheye
and Pistach and say with a smile: 'You really think I crazy,
eh?'

'Well . . .' Fisheye said, stalling, caught, surprised.

Strong enough so he could, still smiling, say: 'Not full
crazy, sorta crazy? Eh?'

'Yes, sorta crazy.'

That broke the ice for a time. For a time he began again
out of his loneliness, his caring, to seek them out, taking
to them tit-bits of his thoughts, listening to them, playing

knock out ping-pong games with them; but he felt himself an eavesdropper on their conversations.

They had grown away from each other. When they did talk, all they did was repeat the memories of the Corner, of those days; they would go no further. Even the adventure of the two days was difficult to deal with. Only Fisheye really kept talking about them. It was as if he had decided to live on those memories alone, not so much to learn from them, but to recall them so that they would celebrate himself, so that he would say: 'And I come up behind them, the gun in my hand, and I say, Nobody ain't moving on. . . .' In jail he was all right. He got what he wanted, and he survived. He was for the first time in his life a survivor. It was as if having prepared himself to die and being robbed of that death, he had made a kind of peace, like the one Terry and Reds had made long ago with the Project work: you take care of me, I take care of you. But, there was a difference.

'We change,' Aldrick said, explaining aloud what they all knew, felt was responsible for their difficulties in communication.

'Yes,' Fisheye said. 'Me, I'm smarter. I know now that you have to have real power, and if you don't have it, man, you have to survive with them that have it. It's a joke, man, this business of being bad, a bad John. That is a old long time thing. That gone out with the biscuit drum and the three note boom. Now a man have to learn how to live.'

'Live? But you don't see, man, that is just what they want us to do. They want us to give up, to surrender because we can't win. Because we don't have power to beat them don't mean we can't be people.'

'You wrong, man, what should be, and what is is two different things. Man, you don't know how much things I see. I tired now. I just want to get a cigarette to smoke, and play a few games, and let time pass so I could go out into the world again. . . . Listen, you know why we play a mas'? Why? Is because a man alone, that is all he could play. That

is all a man alone could do. And I play one of the best mas'
that ever play in Port of Spain. Remember your uncle,
Freddie? I know, cause I see your uncle when he was at his
best with his dragon; I see Joe Prengay and Sonny Miller
karay in a stickfight ring; I was in Calvary Hill band
when we was fighting Tokyo and Casablanca. I was in
town, in the middle of it, when we clash with Desperadoes.
I see Batman and Ozzie and Barker and Baron and Big Sax
and Mastifay and Zigilee. I see all of them. Alone, all a man
could do is play a mas'. . . . Hey! Is my game.'

And Fisheye got up, not with too great a hurry, to take
his turn at the ping-pong table.

15

The Dragon Can't Dance

Sylvia turned from the stand-pipe to the tub below the governor plum tree, enduring still in the yard, shelter for the washtub, pole for the clothesline, bearing still its little green berries that seemed to disappear before they turned the purple of ripeness; and turning still, her body moving in a loose easy unharnessed freedom, dancing to a calypso strummed inside her on a double second pan, a soft grumbling dancing, the movements printing the outline of her panties against her dress, she lifted her head to the sky and the clouds to see whether she should hang out her washing, and glimpsed out of the corner of her eyes this figure, this male blur of dark colours coming softly past the fence of woodslats and stubs of hibiscus, drying now and dying and knotted and old, the more enduring of them sending out thin, willowy stems of a pale anaemic green, that threw out a flower now and then to startle the Yard, to make Miss Cleothilda, who had cultivated an eye for such things, the small miracles of Alice Street, say: 'Oh gosh! Look, the hibiscus bloom! We must water it.' And thenceforth, for a few days at least, begin to favour the blossoming tree with a few cups of water, as if she first needed from it the fact of its blooming to justify wetting the earth around its parched and gasping roots; and she turned again, thinking, saying: 'Oh gosh! Is Aldrick! Is Aldrick,' the thought, sight of him sending a chilling melting thrilling through her flesh, flinging her back seven years, past the anger of her hurt pride, to Aldrick in his little room, making his dragon costume, and to herself,

the girl Sylvia at seventeen standing before his door making
him the offer of herself, that old self: the innocence, the
faith that she must have held once, the belief that she could
live on love alone; and she felt herself touched in a tender
place that she had built a wall around during these years;
felt in herself hardness and wisdom and age that she only
now realized she had acquired.

She stood there with this wistful smile on her face,
watching her old self, the young Sylvia, seeing Aldrick
coming towards her with his same old, smooth, unhurried
walk, half rolling, half dancing, with his eyes looking at
her, into her, through her, past her to the two of them
seven years back when she was seventeen and he was the
king dragon on the Hill; and wondering whether he had
heard the exclamation sight of him had tugged out of her,
embarrassed a little at what he might believe it meant, but,
already thinking to steady herself: It don't mean nothing
. . . is just that is so long I ain't see him . . . is just my
surprise, not even welcome, really . . . just my surprise . . .

All the way up to Alice Street, Aldrick, returning now to
the Hill after five years in prison, had received from people
who saw him, a welcome that at the beginning and briefly
he had thought was one for a returning hero, but it soon
dawned on him that it was more accurately the consoling
greeting for a defeated warrior from a band of deserters who
had long made peace with the enemy. Their purpose, he
felt, in buying him drinks, fêting him with fried chicken
and juke box music at Freddie's snackette, was so that they
could say to him over and over again in all their different
tones of consolation and jubilation: 'That is why we
deserted. Long, even before you came to know it, we knew
that we couldn't win. You had to fight and be conquered to
understand; we knew it in advance. We don't have the
ammunition, they are too strong; victory against them is a
dream we have no chance of achieving. Welcome now to
reality, welcome now to the Hill of accommodation.'

It was Carnival season; and they were filled with that

power that gripped them in that time, that boisterous generosity. They shook his hands. They slapped his shoulders. They pushed women on him 'Have a good time!' they said. But the only wrong thing was that he didn't believe he had been defeated. And he would have told them so. He would have told them 'I am here to live,' but they kept on interrupting him, insisting that he dance with a girl, take another drink, listen to Philo's calypsos on the juke box, and in order to be polite – how could he refuse a drink with fellars he hadn't seen for five years? – but also waiting for a lull in their conversation, a silence from them so he could speak his piece, trying to fashion a way in which he could say, 'I am not conquered,' without wounding, bruising too roughly their own sensibility, without abusing their hospitality, he sat there while they flaunted with every gesture, their older wisdom. So he decided that he would put off confronting them with his side of the story. And he tried. He tried to drink the beers and eat the fried chicken, and he even danced with one of the girls, Molly, a tall, strong looking girl with huge thighs and a very short print dress. He tried, but he was like a dead weight on the table, a dead spirit in the midst of this festival of defeat.

'What happen to him, he ain't dancing,' the buxom Molly complained, coming around behind his chair and resting her two hands on his neck. 'What happen, Slim?' softly, invitingly. She was a new girl and didn't know his name.

'But I dance already.'

'Well, dance again. We come here to have a good time, not so? And how we going to have a good time if you don't dance?'

' You playing mas'?' he asked her, trying to change the subject. 'What you playing?'

'What mas' I playing? Devil,' she said. 'The band playing devils.'

'Devil!' an exclamation jumped out of him. 'You mean

people playing devil again?' Maybe he had misread the signs. If people were playing devil . . . if they were expressing the wish to be devil, evil, powerful, then maybe a new spirit was rising again. Oh Jesus, he thought, Oh Jesus!

'Two thousand strong,' she said.

Two thousand people playing devil in Port of Spain. He smiled.

'Not real devil, you know. Fancy devil, with lamé and silk and satin. Pretty devil.'

Pretty devil! Pretty devil. In silk and satin.

'Oh ho. I used to play a dragon,' he said. 'But it wasn't pretty. It was a real dragon, with fire coming out the mouth and claws on the hands.'

'Oh . . . you is the fellar . . . Aldrick, was in jail for the riot. They talk 'bout you. Well come and dance, man,' she said, as if she knew him better now. 'Come, dragon.'

And he kinda wished he felt to dance. He wished that the old music, the old feeling was in him, to sit in the rum shop and drink beers and talk loud with fellars and argue about calypso and Carnival and which is the best playing steelband, and make rough jokes and dance with a woman, as when he was the dragon.

But just as he had found it difficult to tell it to the men that he had made no accommodation with defeat, that, indeed, he was not defeated, so he was finding it difficult to tell this girl that he didn't feel to dance. It was a new sadness. It was a great sadness.

The girl, Molly, had come around to his side, and must have seen it on his face, the pain, for she said, 'All right, Slim,' very gently, patting his cheeks, and with her regrets. 'All right, Slim.'

All right, Slim . . . and he had slipped away then and mounted the Hill, watching, in the dulled sun, the shacks of box-board and wood slabs, their bright paint dulled by seasons, poised on short pillars and set on the hillside in the same crazy formation he had left them in five years ago, waiting, it seemed, for the start of a bizarre race, and at a whistle blast or pistol shot they would all take off, go avalanching down the Hill to crash into Port of Spain. He had walked, the dust and dirt smell in his nostrils, listening to the place that, away from the juke box blare, with the steelband practising sounding far away, contained that quality of peacefulness, of the quiet, of an old childless widow who, expecting neither husband nor children, chuckled now and then at memories; and he felt himself a stranger, one who had come home, and one who could no longer be at home here, and here was his home . . . All right, Slim. All right. . . .

'How you?' he asked softly, respectfully, almost with apology, standing a distance off from Sylvia as if waiting to be invited to come more into her presence.

'I say you dead,' she said.

Dead! That was the Hill for you. It hurt with every word. With its most tender feeling it hammered nails into your flesh.

'I come to see you.'

She looked at him, conscious of time, her ageing, her wisdom, looked at him as if he were a mirror in which she was studying her reflection. 'I get old, eh?'

He shook his head. 'You can't get old.'

She smiled, flattered. 'You spend a long time in prison for that stupidness. It didn't do nothing for nobody. The government started to fix the streets up here, and they give some fellars work on a Project, then they stop. Why you all do that?'

'It just happen,' he said.

'Some people was glad though.'

'They was glad?'

She ignored him. 'I was there. I went to listen to hear what it was about, but I didn't understand one thing. You didn't see me? I was right to the front, on the pavement. I hear you talking. I didn't know you coulda talk so. Everybody was surprised you coulda talk so.'

'I wanted to say I love you,' he said. 'I wanted to shout it for everybody to hear.'

'Why you didn't do it? 'Fraid?'

'Yes. But I ain't afraid now.'

She turned to her bucket with the washed clothes in it, took out a garment and began to hang it on the line. 'You know your old room gone,' she said, looking in the direction of the shack in which he had lived. 'Two fellars lived there since you gone. The first one moved out last year, and the other one there right now.'

'I ain't frightened now,' he said.

'And Pariag – you remember the Indian fellar with the thin wife – he gone from the Yard. The shop at the corner is his own now. Miss Cleothilda still here as the rock of ages. She gone to town today, but she should be coming back just now. She sure will be surprised to see you. And I guess you know that your friend Philo is a big star now,' she said, taking another garment from the bucket and pausing with a clothesclip in her mouth, and resuming even before she had properly removed it from her mouth: 'He live in Diego Martin, singing calypso all over the world, going to America and England. He is a big shot. Now and again he does come here and look for Cleo . . . I hanging out these clothes on this line and I feel it will rain. You think it will come, the rain?'

'You ever think about leaving this place, leaving here?' he asked.

And, still hanging out clothes, as if she hadn't heard the question: 'And now I living by myself. I have the room Pariag used to live in. I fix it up. . . . And Ma in hospital. I have to go and see her this evening.'

'You know,' he said, as she paused with a clothesclip in her mouth, her tippingtoe lifting her dress up her thighs. 'You know, I didn't know nothing about life before. . . . Life was only my dragon long ago.'

'And the little boy, Basil, the boy who used to come by you to make the dragon costume – if you see how tall the little boy get. He is a recruit now in the Police Force.'

'Now I know I ain't a dragon. . . . Funny, eh? Years. And now I know I is more than just to play a masquerade once a year for two days, to live for two days,' he said. 'It have life for us to live, girl. Life.'

She looked at him now, her pose of casualness dented, her eyes wary, almost afraid as that first time when she had come with the white dress and the oversized shoes and the ribbon in her hair to offer herself to him. 'Why you come back here for?' she asked, her eyes wide, on her face a grimace.

'To see you. I come back to see you.'

She looked at him closely. She sighed.

'You didn't tell me about Guy. What about him?' he said.

'Come inside out the sun,' she said.

'You want a drink?' she asked him, in that same half frightened tone. 'All I have is rum, and orange juice.' They were now inside.

As he went to sit down, he saw that she was trembling. 'Rum, and a little orange juice,' he said.

What was once one big room was now made two smaller ones by a hardboard partition. The one he sat in, the living room, was clean and polished, and had a lot of knick-knacks all over the place. A large straw mat almost took up the entire floor.

She opened the refrigerator and took out the orange juice.

'You have a nice place here,' he said. He had seen the radio and TV and stereo and the chairs and the knick-knacks, and the framed pictures of cut-outs from magazines, and prints of a couple local scenes, and there was a picture of Bless This House over the door, that he hadn't seen when he was coming in. She expected the compliment.

'I comfortable here,' she said, almost as a plea. 'I have everything I want.'

'This rum tasting good,' he said, sipping his drink to

cover his sadness; for, yes, he could see that Sylvia in her way had arrived, that, at least, she could feel she had arrived; her own clean, polished room with almost every available modern convenience. She was too wise now for love.

'You didn't tell me about Guy,' he said.

'What *you* want to know?' she asked, her tone agressive again, seeking shelter in accusation.

But before he could say anything, he heard the sound of Miss Cleothilda's voice calling Sylvia. He looked at Sylvia, as the voice drew nearer.

'Sylvia, if you know how things dear in Port of Spain. I went to buy the sequins for my jacket, and if you know what price they selling them . . . Hey! (she saw him then) You have visitors.' And when he turned. 'Hi! Is you!'

'Aldrick just drop in. We just this minute sit down here,' Sylvia said.

'Well, if you have visitors, I better go. You could see me any time,' she said, not moving from the door.

'No. Come in.'

'No. I will stay too long. Let me go and put down these things . . . Well' (to Aldrick), pushing her hand over the half door: 'Shake my hand. Is a long time.'

Aldrick stood, reached out, and shook hands with her, bearing that swift studied scrutiny that Miss Cleothilda had learned to effect so that no detail might miss her, so that she would be able to say, almost with reluctance: 'You looking well. Jail agree with you. . . . And, you know, last night . . . Yes, it was last night . . . I dream you. I didn't tell you, Sylvia?'

She had aged rapidly. Whatever prop that had been propping up the muscles of her face had collapsed now, and neither the powder nor the rouge would be able to hold them. Her hair was still done in two long plaits that, because of the dye, showed no trace of grey; it was as if she had contrived to go through life, even towards her grave, as a schoolgirl.

'I dream how you come here with a rope in your hands and was pulling down the shop, my shop; but you don't have to pull it down. It gone to the dogs already. I find it so funny that you should want to pull down my shop. But, you don't have to pull it down, Aldrick; it pull down already. Sylvia ain't tell you the Indian boy, Pariag, buy the shop at the corner . . . (looking at Sylvia) Well, he buy it. I ain't vex with him. I ain't vex at all,' she said, without any joy, with a kind of knowing, as if she, unhappily, could prophesy the end of Pariag and his shop. 'I ain't jealous. He young, and is a free country; so if he come to this town, to this Hill, and put up a shop for people to buy from him, I is the last one to say anything ill. The only reason I mention it at all is because last night I dream how you come with this long long rope and tie the shop and try to pull it down, and I want you to know that it pull down already, and I tired.

'I really tired, you know. I find these days I ain't able with people. I find things ain't have no value these days, and the little value they have they losing faster than babies borning on this Hill. This place going to the dogs. Long ago when you and Philo was living here, it had decent people on this Hill – poor, but decent. Now is the last crumbs and dust of people here, doing anything for a dollar. They racketeering, they robbing, they shooting. No! They ain't using knife again. Is like since Fisheye pick up that gun and stick up the police and kidnap their jeep, guns sprouting all over town. Prayer is all remain. Prayer. I don't know what woulda been my condition if I didn't used to pray,' she said, making the sign of the cross over her body. 'Battoo's Funeral Home woulda long carried me away. And, with Sylvia going away from here in a month or two, I can't imagine what I would do . . .' And, as Aldrick glanced at Sylvia: 'She ain't tell you? You ain't tell him, Sylvia? I don't want to tell him your business, you know; though when you give out the invitations everybody will know. You shame? You shouldn't shame, you know. Guy is a City

Councillor now. He is a man treat you good from the beginning: TV, radio, fridge, stereo, dress, show. He old, is true. Everybody have to get old – people say I old too – you don't have to love him now. Love will come, and if it never come, at least you will be comfortable; for one thing you know about him is he will take care of you, which is more than you could say for these young fellars buzzing around behind you. The boy Raymond good looking, but where he going to put you? Now and again he make a pair of sandals for one of his friends. He ain't working nowhere. How you going to live so? You tell him 'bout Raymond? You know 'bout Raymond?'

Aldrick shook his head, his eyes on Sylvia.

'You ain't tell him 'bout Raymond?'

'We hardly start to talk anything,' Sylvia answered.

'Well, I better shut my big mouth and go. I will see you later.'

Then, moving away, she turned back and came to the door. 'But the reason I saying all this is so he will know he can't come here just so, breeze in here after five years in prison and tantalize your brain. What you could do for her, Aldrick? I talking plain. Tell me, what you could give her?' And, without waiting for an answer, as if she was satisfied now that she had had her say, she turned from the door.

'I was going to tell you,' Sylvia said, after a while. 'Is time for me to settle down, make something of my life, have children. I ain't getting younger, you know. And I tired with these fellars I offer myself to. I tired listening to them talk, and can't see nothing.'

'So you getting married to Guy?'

'Yes.'

He was quiet now, watching about the room, thinking.

'You want another drink?'

'No thank you.'

'What you could give me?' she asked suddenly, challengingly.

'Yourself,' he said.

'You know, you change,' she said.

He put the glass to his head and let a piece of ice from it fall into his mouth. He didn't say anything.

'You sure you don't want another drink?'

He shook his head.

'What you come here for? Eh? What?'

'I'm sorry,' he said.

'Where you going to go?' she asked him.

'I'll get a place somewhere. I'll do something.'

'You have money?'

He shook his head. 'Is okay, I'll get through.'

'You know you crazy,' she said, admonishing him as if she were an older sister. 'You think you going to go and live and not pay rent like long ago. Things change, you know.'

She got up and went inside. When she returned, he was standing. He saw that she had a twenty dollar bill in her hand.

'Take this,' she said, offering him the money. 'Don't look at me, take it. You could at least buy cigarettes. Take it. Don't say anything. Just take it.'

She stuffed it into his shirt pocket.

'And go,' she said, tears beginning to reach her voice. 'I is nearly a married woman. And don't come back.'

'Keep well,' he said. He said it again, as a plea, 'Keep well, eh.'

She followed him to the door.

'You's a real princess, girl,' he said, pausing at the door.

She pushed him outside. 'Goodbye! Goodbye!'

'. . . And all this polish and glitter is not you. You is a queen, girl; and this room, pretty as it is, is not you, is not your end. And you young still, and you don't have to hide yourself underneath no polish and in no room. You don't want nobody to take care of you, to hide you, to imprison you. You want to be a self that is free, girl; to grow, girl; to be, to be yourself, girl.'

'Aldrick, goodbye!'

'You's a queen, girl."

'Goodbye! Shake my hand!'

She held out her hand stiffly, her head looking into the distance over his shoulder. He took her hand. He leaned and kissed her lightly on the cheek. He turned and walked away. He didn't want to look back; but, he heard Miss Cleothilda's voice calling out: 'We'll send you an invitation,' triumphantly, as if at the end of it all she had won; that Sylvia was on her way to being a new Miss Cleothilda, diverted from her genius, her talents, her gifts; she would settle down with Guy on this or on some other hill or valley in the island, with her furniture and knick-knacks and her plants and she would have a dog, and her husband would die long before she did and leave her a widow.

'We'll have the steelband playing, roti, rum, bacchanal! We going to have a fête big as Carnival,' Miss Cleothilda called out.

He didn't reply. He walked on, not wanting to turn his head. Then, he looked back, and saw Sylvia standing stiffly in the yard, her head held straight, her hands at her sides. He didn't wave. She didn't wave either. And then she waved, thrusting both hands into the air in a saucy, brave and affirming sign. And it struck him: maybe she has not given up hope for life, for living. Maybe she had not so much chosen Guy as refused the impotence of dragons.

Maybe Miss Cleothilda had misread the situation. Sylvia had not surrendered; she was simply turning, turning from the dragon to herself. Guy was just in between. But, marriage . . . ? Marriage! A fear gripped him, and as if to throw it off, he turned and waved again, this time with both hands, signalling faith in her and a joy in the moment, signalling as a dear friend, a lover, who is going on before to be joined later by her. In truth, he felt to rush back to her and hold her in his hands and lift her up and carry her away with him; but, he had come to Sylvia, not to claim her, but to help her claim herself; and he felt the need for the strength and the faith, the love, to allow her to make that claim for her own self.

Aldrick walked down the Hill with brave reluctance, holding in his brain the consoling thought: one is saved only by one's self, as a faith, a hope, understanding and generosity and love for Sylvia and humankind. And as he walked past Pariag's shop, this thought spinning in his brain, he stopped, paused before the shop as before the door of one who might have been an old friend if they had managed to make friends earlier; and he remembered the thin Indian fellar and the new Humber bicycle, and the sign he wanted painted, and the day he walked, marched, tall with the bicycle through the street, past the Corner; and he realized that he did not really know Pariag; though, he might have known him if he had known himself. Pariag had stumbled into the Yard, and without welcome, had been asked to bear the burden of a battle he did not know was his own, that was never shown him to be his own, and which could not be shown either, because none of them in the Yard could explain it – not he, nor Philo, nor Miss Olive, nor Miss Caroline – since they could not explain it to themselves, since it was something lived for generations, lived so long that it had become a life, beyond explanation. And even if they could have explained it, could they have offered him that life? Could they have offered him the dragon, Carnival, rebellion, the possession of nothing?

For a moment Aldrick was tempted to go in and talk to Pariag, but he felt that there was nothing to explain, really. Each man – Pariag included – had the responsibility for his own living, had the responsibility for the world he lived in, and to claim himself and to grow and to grow and to grow. No. There was nothing to explain to him.

Aldrick walked down the Hill. He wondered what he would do now. He thought of sign painting. He would become a sign painter. He thought of some signs he could paint: Beware of the dog! No spitting! Trespassers will be

prosecuted according to the Law! No obscene language!
Wet Paint! Men at Work! He had to laugh. Maybe he could
paint some new signs, signs of life, of hope, of love, of
affirming, and let his own living match and mirror them.

He walked past Freddie's snackette and felt strong enough
to look in. Turning back to the street, he saw a fellar in a
red car driving up the Hill – Jesus! That is . . . looking
just like, just like . . . but, no. It wasn't Philo. And his
mind went back to the old days and the Yard and the
Corner, and to Fisheye and Philo, and Sylvia, and he
smiled, the smile warming him, and he didn't regret
nothing. He just felt this sweet, hard, this beautiful
gladness to have lived that life and to be here now, walking
down the street, alive, and ready to go on. He didn't regret
nothing. For he was a good dragon, when he was a
dragon – the best, the best in Port of Spain, in Trinidad,
in the world. He was the best dragon in the whole fucking
world. And just for that he felt he would like to sit down
with the fellars who had shared those days with him, with
Fisheye and Philo, over a drink, and say: 'We was good. We
was the best. Come, let's go again.'

16

The Shopkeeper

Aldrick didn't know it, but Pariag had caught sight of him as he paused in front Pariag's shop before he turned from entering it and moved on. Pariag didn't say anything about it, not even to Dolly who had witnessed the event, for he did not want her to see his disappointment and concern, since he knew that she believed that he was too important now to allow such a thing to touch him.

The truth was that it did. It brought back to him a sense of loss and a kind of aloneness that over the last five six years had surprised him at odd moments, bringing a kind of panic questioning of himself: *What it is you doing? What you doing? What you doing?* questions which, while they touched the sorest centre in himself, he had allowed himself to neglect, seeing that the shop in which he was ceaselessly at work had the appearance of an answer the whole world would understand, if not applaud. Now, it settled into him, this sense of loss and the aloneness, as a pain no one knew of, but one that he was sometimes grateful that he could still feel, as a nostalgia for the earlier purpose that had moved him out of the bosom of his family and New Lands to encounter men like Fisheye and Aldrick in Port of Spain.

What worried him was not that Aldrick had moved on, but that Aldrick had paused. Aldrick had stopped before his shop. This meant that for a moment at least Aldrick had considered entering it. Why had he moved on?

For the remainder of the day, Pariag, puzzling over the meaning of what Aldrick had done, moved about the shop with a soft, slow, distracted dreaminess which Miss Caroline, purchasing a few items of groceries, was given an opportunity to interpret.

'The madame giving you worries or what? I ask you for half pound saltfish and, look, you giving me five pounds of onion!'

Dolly was near by, and they had all laughed, but, with her laughter dying, Dolly had looked at him. He wondered about that look: was it concern for him, or was she wondering how much such mistakes had cost them in dollars and cents that day: and the question flashed across his mind with a quick panic winking, a red light flashing at an intersection late in the night: *What it is you doing? What you doing? What you doing?* And his mind went back to Aldrick.

And then it was night. They had closed the shop and were upstairs in the living room: Pariag eating and half looking at TV and the news, and Dolly in a kind of separate aloneness, watching TV and nursing the last child, the third girl.

'I hope he don't think that because I have shop now if he come in we can't talk,' Boya said, trying to sound tough, but failing; so that he was moved to support his attempt: 'Shop don't make a man.'

'Why that should worry you?' Dolly said. 'You don't have to beg them for their friendship again, or for anything.'

'We could talk,' Pariag said. 'People could talk. It have things for us to talk about.'

'What you going to talk about with him? Prison?'

Pariag didn't reply immediately. Then he tried again: 'You know what worrying me,' he said, 'is that I paused too. I see him standing up there, and same time I thinking to call him, and wondering what kinda welcome to give him. I had a chance to call him in. I didn't do it. I paused too. Just like him – and moved on.'

Dolly was going to get up, but she leaned back in her chair, the child, finishing nursing, half asleep in her arms.

'Boya, sometimes I don't understand you. I thought you say you done with Creole people.'

'You know, is how he come so sudden,' Pariag said, his voice knotting and straining, 'so outa the blue. If I wasn't so surprised to see him – if I myself wasn't so sure that he was going to come in, I woulda call him in. . . . Unless, maybe I was frighten.'

'But they don't have any power to insult you again, Boya. You don't owe them nothing. I don't see whether if you call him or he call you, why that should worry you.'

He smiled patiently, forcing back a groan; and Dolly got up to take the sleeping child to her crib and he put his head in his two hands.

Later, Pariag walked out on to his verandah overlooking the street, and he listened to the night sounds, the cars and dogs and music from radios and the steelband practising for Carnival, and he felt the steamy heat of the night, and the smell of the street, of the Hill, came to him, and he thought about his daughters and of his grandfather who had died a year before, and of New Lands and his parents and his uncle Ramlochan who had taken a new wife, a young girl who everybody was cold with because they said she had married him for his property, and Dolly came out on the verandah, softly and with an air of apology and said to him gently, 'It on. You coming to see it?' and he turned and followed her inside and sat down in front the TV and watched the Indian Talent show, watched the Master of Ceremonies who, introducing the singers and dancers with smooth grand gestures and an exaggerated Indian accent, reminded him of Balliram announcing Indian pictures, though this man was more polished, more grave and righteous, less humorous. The show itself was too smooth, too easy. Its triumph was too much of a foregone conclusion. It tired him. And now he saw something that was always missing for him in these shows. He realized what it was now, for the first time. It lacked the guts of the struggle he, Pariag, had lived and Dolly had lived and his

father and his uncle Ramlochan. It didn't have the
sugarcane and the cow dung in it and the roasted peanuts
and the boiled and fried channa in a basket round the
Savannah with Colts playing Malvern (Maple done get licks
already). It jingled with jewels, and leaves fell and there
was perfume; but it didn't have bottles in it. It didn't have
Balliram and Vishnu on the bottles truck at five o'clock in
the morning, and Seenath, Bali and Ramjohn playing all
fours in the pavilion of New Lands Recreation ground. It
didn't have his struggle with the Hill in it. Yet, as distant
as it was from him, it was close, very close to him, and he
was glad to have it as one is glad to have the memory of a
self; he just wished that there was more of himself in it.

He turned to Dolly, to say something, but she wasn't
looking, and he turned back to the TV screen.

It was things like these he wanted to talk about now.
But, that is your guts, man. That deeper than your guts.
That is your heart you talking about.

Yes, he would like to talk about his guts from his guts.
He would like to talk from his heart about things close to
his heart. He tried to think when last he had talked about
more than the cost of flour and rice and saltfish. 'Is so
long,' he thought, since I talk to anybody. So long. They
had pushed him back. He had tried, but they had forced
him back. But, could he continue to remain so . . . so cut
off from risking himself? Shouldn't he try again?

He wondered if Aldrick would listen to him now. And he
thought: maybe that is why he had paused. But, then, why
had he moved on?

The show ended and Pariag remained seated, silent.
Dolly suppressed a yawn, but sensing Pariag's mood, she
decided to stay in the room with him, though she realized
that in moments like these he entered an area of himself
from which she was excluded.

I wish we was luckier, Pariag was thinking. All of us: me
and Aldrick and Fisheye and Philo and the Yard and the
Hill. I wish we was luckier with each other.

I wish . . . I wish I was just beginning now, just coming into the Yard for the first time, with things in place: with Fisheye and Aldrick and Cleothilda in place . . . No. No. I wish I had choose myself to represent myself. I wish I had come with me, my own spirit and soul and grief and love and say, Look me! Look me!

And he wasn't satisfied with that either.

. . . I wish I did walk with a flute or a sitar, and walk in right there in the middle of the steelband yard where they was making new drums, new sounds, a new music from rubbish tins and bits of steel and oil drums, bending the iron over fire, chiselling out new notes. New notes. I wish I woulda go in there where they was making their life anew in fire, with chisel and hammer, and sit down with my sitar on my knee and say: Fellars, this is me, Pariag from New Lands. Gimme the key! Give me the Do Re Mi. Run over the scale. Leh We Fa Sol La! Gimme the beat, lemme beat! Listen to these strings. And let his music cry too, and join in the crying. Let it scream too. Let it sing 'bout Dolly in the old ramshackle house in Tabaquite, with the smell of green grass and cow dung, let it laugh with Seenath, Bali and Ramjohn playing all fours, singing bullseyes in the pavilion of New Lands recreation ground, let it groan with the groaning weight of tons and tons of sugarcane on top his grandfather's frail shoulders. Let it smile with his uncle Ramlochan sitting at the window with his dark shades on. And he smiled, thinking of Miss Cleothilda and her All o' we is one. No. We didn't have to melt into one. I woulda be me for my own self. A beginning. A self to go in the world with, with something in my hands to give. We didn't have to melt into one. They woulda see me.

'They woulda see me,' he said, this time aloud, so that Dolly who, for all her good intentions, was dozing off at just that instant, hearing his voice, would say, a little too loudly and abruptly, 'Boya, you calling me?'

'Girl,' he said, touched and amused at her pretence of

being awake, but more touched than amused, 'don't punish yourself. Come, go and sleep in your bed. Come!' And he got up and took her by the hand, 'Come.'

'Yes,' she said, drowsy, smiling, her upper teeth jutting, more relaxed now and closer to him in spirit, and, to him, the girl who had looked at him and had seen the dreams in him, the more than country in him.

They were changing for bed. He felt he could risk himself, expose his weakness, his caring.

'You know they never see me.'

'Boya, they see you!' she said as if it was something she had known for a long long time, but was forced to tell him now. 'Everybody see you. With the shop and everything, everybody see you. You want them to see you more than they see you.'

'They never really see me.'

'But, you here . . . With the shop . . . They must see you.'

And then he understood something very new. 'You right.'

Yes, they *had* seen him. But now, he thought, they would never see him; for they believed that they had seen him already. That was the hard part.

'You know what is the hard part?' he said, sitting on the bed.

'What is the hard part?'

'They see one part of me and they take that to be the whole me. They take the part of me that they see, that—'

'That they want to see.'

He paused again. Again she had hit on something. 'The part that I show them . . . I wanted to show them me; but, only a part I show them.'

'The part that they allow you to show them.'

'What you show is what you is, Dolly.' He sounded resigned.

Her voice leaped out of her anxious, protective, authoritative:

'You is more, Boya. More than what you show them. I is more than what I show you, not so?'

Pariag became very quiet.

Dolly said, 'You not vex I say that?'

He shook his head. 'Everybody is more than what they show. That is why we have to live.' He sighed, then fixed his pillow in place.

'. . . But how you make someone know you, who know you too long and don't know you at all?' After a long pause he answered the question himself. 'When you expose your whole self to them.'

'I see now,' Dolly said. 'You shoulda talk to Aldrick in truth.'

But he was thinking of something else, *seeing* something else.

'*We* have to start to live, Dolly, you and me.'

'*Me* and you?' Dolly asked, her voice choking. '*Me* and you?'

What did he know of this woman? She had tears in her eyes and she was looking at him with a kind of astonishment and respect, the same way she had looked at him when he had said, 'You going to have to live in Port of Spain.'

Port of Spain? He smiled then, thinking back to the Boya of those days, and thinking, Port of Spain? Port of Spain! recalling to mind a calypso by Philo that was the road march a few years ago.

17

The Calypsonian

Philo sat out on the verandah of his house in Diego Martin, and looked out across his lawn, watched the neighbouring house with its lawn and TV antenna and part bred German shepherd dog, saw beyond that the other houses which differed only in colour – some brown, some cream, others light green; mild colours under the surrounding green mountains – and for the first time since coming here to live, he was struck by the newness and sameness of everything: the houses, lawns, motor cars in garages along whose walls the ivy sitting in their new ceramic pots had not yet begun to climb. It was Sunday and the men of the neighbourhood had come to the front of their houses, in short pants and with slippers on to wash down their cars and to exchange waves and smiles, a ritual in which they were secure only because everybody performed it.

Watching now, *seeing* now, and overtaken by a kind of horror, he felt a calypso on the edge of his brain:

The new people so new, you know, nobody
Don't know who is who
They so all the same, all of them carry
The same kinda name
Same kinda dog, same kinda wife, all of them living
The same kinda life.

Mr John and Mr Harry coming home drunk
Went to sleep in each other's house
Live for years nobody complain

Until one night drunk again
The two fellars make back the exchange.

Philo sat back, a smile coming on to his face, thinking: 'Jesus Lord! I find them out! I find them out!' believing that this knowledge on its own, this 'finding them out', set him apart from his neighbours and above them:

> *Cause the same kinda dress, same kinda shoe*
> *Same hair cut, same hair do*
> *I hear it is true, they all caress their wife*
> *On the same night too . . .*

not yet thinking that this was his home too, that this was where he had come from Calvary Hill to, thinking instead, a smile twinkling in his brain: 'Lemme write this down quick!' getting up, to go to his desk for a pen and paper, in that smooth careful motion he used whenever he felt something coming.

It would be at his desk, just as he was getting up after making his hurried jottings, that his eyes fell upon the gold-edged card, the invitation to the wedding of M. A. Guy and Sylvia. He had read it four times already since getting it from Cleothilda a few days ago, but he picked it up and took it with him to the verandah, intending to read it again, as if he still wasn't satisfied that he had received the information it intended to transmit, as if it contained not a clear message that could be conveyed straight forward and in one reading, but rather, a parable to unpuzzle.

Sylvia and Guy! Sylvia!

Maybe it was because he had seen Sylvia grow up there in the Yard on Alice Street, seen in her the spirit, the fire, the speed; the beauty that somehow in her was not a female weapon to be used to bend men to her will, to advance herself in the world, but was, instead, the declaration of a faith in life and a promise to life, that promise which shone on the faces of some children even through the fogs of slums, making of their poor rags a halo the better to make them shine, be seen, to make the world step back a pace before them to watch them go by, move on, illuminated and doomed by that aura that sets apart for the gaze of ordinary people the most beautiful of anything, of fruit or flower or fowl or beast, so that only the rashest and most irreverent would think to pluck it from its rootage. It was this quality in her, more than any lack of attraction or absence of desire that had been most restraining on himself, that had made her for him more than just a female person to be pursued, captured and fucked; so that while his body had cried out with wanting he had stepped back that pace before her and watched her go by; so that it had to be Guy. It had to be Guy. Aldrick saw it in her and he was afraid; even the young men buzzing around the Yard sensed it: only Guy. Only Guy of all the men would be brazen enough and rash and blind as not to see, not to realize that her very desirability placed her above ordinary desiring. Only Guy was so clever, so smart and dense and cunning to believe that all the men had pulled back from her just so he could have her. Like the small boy who doubles back and steals the small bird from its nest after he had heard the others, no less hunter than he, touched by its beauty, even when the nest itself was so vulnerable to pillage, say: 'We will not take this one.' Like that small boy who has learned nothing but the grabbing and the scheming, who listens to the others say, 'We will not take this one', and himself says nothing – so that after he had doubled back and taken the small bird for himself he would be able to say, with what he believed was truthfulness, 'I didn't say anything about not taking it.' So, Guy, without any competition at all, almost as if she were an ordinary girl, just any other seventeen-year-old Hill girl, captured her.

But even after Guy had coaxed her up his steps, she had remained in Philo's eyes symbol and flesh of that faith in life and promise to life, her very vulnerability making her more chaste, more virgin, more – if you want – sainted, untarnished even when wearing the costume that Aldrick might have bought for her if he had the guts, the craziness, to leap beyond his fears and caring and take her and let what happen happen. So, over the years he had watched Guy with her as a kind of contradiction, a kind of accident, one of those things that tumbled into being to, as his mother used to say, 'fulfil righteousness', that would soon, however, come to its end, leaving her inviolate and chaste and voluptuous to live and symbolize her promise and life. . . . Marriage to Guy was a horse of a different colour.

Not, as he told Cleothilda, after she had handed him the invitation that Sylvia had left with her for him, not that Guy would wilfully set out to make any new demands on her, except the very reasonable one that she appear upright and proper as befitting the wife of a City Councillor, but, simply because he was blind and unfeeling to anything that did not bring in money, that could not be sold at a profit, he would destroy her without even knowing it; for how could a man who is blind (and foolish too) avoid trampling the plants in a garden through which he walks believing it to be a highway?

'Even if he love her?' Cleothilda had asked.

'Love! What is love? And even if you could tell me what love is, what make you believe that Guy could understand that. You believe that Guy know what love is?'

'Well, he tell me, and I telling you just as he say it to me. And he don't owe me nothing, so I don't see why he should want to lie to me. He say: "Cleothilda, I don't know what it is, but I love that girl".'

'And you believe him?'

'You woulda believe him too if he say it to you: "I love that girl",' Cleothilda said, repeating it in a whisper, revealing in her own astonishment that Guy could be so weak, so vulnerable, hinting that his love for Sylvia (if it was that) was something that the girl could exploit to her advantage. 'He will be good for her. He will settle her down.'

'Settle her down?' And Philo had felt affronted by the very thought that Guy could think of taking all that woman, rhythm and that full hope and promise and life, and 'settle her down'.

'Yes,' Miss Cleothilda said, her whispery voice jubilant as if there were some private triumph in it for her. 'Tame her. Put a ring on her finger. That will stop those young men from coming into this Yard on every excuse to watch her, to tempt her – and not one of them have anything, more than the one thing all man have, to offer.'

'Tempt her?'

'So you think is Guy alone she have eyes for?' And, dropping her voice and leaning closer to him so that he was forced to lean towards her to hear: 'You didn't hear about the boy Raymond who was living there in the house when Aldrick was in jail? I didn't tell you she nearly leave Guy and go with him, that she nearly throw sheself away for nothing? I didn't tell you that is I, me, who had to put her to sit down and explain, make her see? All the boy intend was to do is comb up he hair in a big Afro, put on a dashiki, and spin her dreams of Africa. Now and again he make a pair of leather sandals and sell them or give them away to one of his friends. Wouldn't work, cussing the boss anywhere he work, frightening them with his fierce eyes and his beard and his head full of hair and a silver bracelet on his left wrist and small black fist on a string round his neck. I didn't tell you about him? – Maybe is how you don't come here so often again; those young girls taking up your time in Diego Martin and in America and England. Maybe is how when we meet we don't talk so much like we used to talk long ago – Wanted Sylvia to go 'way to Sans Souci and work garden with him. I say, girl, how you could do that? You ain't in Africa; and even in Africa it have cities and clothes and people have to eat, you hear; and here the year is nineteen seventy-one. People done gone to the

moon already. Guy is a City Councillor. You going to go
Sans Souci and plant garden with Raymond? And then on
top that, Raymond want four five woman, because, as he
say, that is the African way. But, the boy ain't working
nowhere. He is chief without no property, and when Guy
finally get him out the house, he was owing four months'
rent. I thought you did know these things.'

'He can't settle her down.'

And Cleothilda, not even hearing him, plunging onward:
'And another man: Talbot. Well, this one is a joke. I don't
know what she see in him to like – or, maybe she was just
sorry for him. Maybe – you ever see a broomstick with a
wrongsided cashew seed on top it, with boots on, and a cap
and a bush jacket with those things – what you call them?
Like army men does have on the shoulders of their
uniforms – epaulettes. Well, that is Talbot. He is a revolu-
tionist, without a penknife in he pocket, fulling Sylvia
head with foolishness about Cuba and China and Vietnam,
want her to go with him on top S'erra Aripo mountains. He
against capitalist. He against the government. The boy
against everything, even dancing. Don't dance, can't dance
face always scowling. "Sylvia, what you see in him? And
girl, when you go with him, where you will live? And
when you will live?" "We don't have nothing now, but after
the revolution," she tell me. After the revolution? After the
revolution. Everything is after the revolution! "Girl, I old
and I know one thing, people does live life every day, today
and today and today, and they have to live it somewhere. So
if you want to go up S'erra Aripo with a pack a biscuits and a
tin a sardines, that is the life you have to prepare to live.
People don't, can't put off living."'

'Oh, they tempt her all the time. Even Aldrick was back
again, just out of prison, his eyes watching her eyes, and
he silent like he find out something that he alone know
about . . .'

'How he looking?'

'Prison agree with him. Quiet, calm, like nothing could

surprise him. When Guy hear that he was here he run quick and set date for the wedding. Things turn out to her advantage. 'Cause if it wasn't for these temptations, he mighta keep her as a outside woman forever, not that a outside woman bad, you know. You know?' she said, slapping his leg, drawing from him a chuckle, so that in a new breath, with a kind of triumphant finality, she would say: 'Now he want to secure her, to make sure that he don't come one day and find her gone with one of these young fellars. I can't blame him.'

And he said, 'She could go with a ring on her finger too.'

'Not in Diego Martin.'

And he said 'Diego Martin? What you mean, not in Diego Martin?'

'Haii! You mean I didn't tell you that he buy a house in Diego Martin and that that is where he carrying she to live?'

And he had said then, that time, two weeks ago: 'Anywhere . . . anywhere on God's earth he carry her, he can't hide her. He can't stop that spirit in her. Not even in a nunnery.' He had said it triumphantly.

And she, probing, still hopeful: 'You mean, not even in Diego Martin?'

'Not there or anywhere it have man and woman and life to live.'

And she, with a bit of surrender in her voice, had said: 'Well, you should know, 'cause is three years now you living in Diego Martin.'

But now, looking across his lawn at the houses imprisoned in this valley, he thought: 'Yes, he could hide her here, bleach her here, domicile her.' The calypso popped back into his brain:

> *'Cause the same smile, the same style.*
> *They don't make nothing, don't shake nothing,*
> *They like robots that wind up and set running.*

He couldn't imagine how he had not seen this before. He couldn't imagine it.

Trips, I made a lotta trips. I wasn't here most o' the time. But, *three* years! Three!

I . . . maybe I took it for granted. Yes, I took it for granted that this was it, that this was the place. It was fine. I didn't inspect it, I just took if for granted. Yes, I took it for granted. Yes. Yes. Yes.

Philo rested down the invitation card gently. He felt upon him a strange, draining tiredness, and he felt old and alone. He thought of himself as the only live soul in a pretty, well laid out cemetery. . . . Or, was he also dead? A chill raced across his insides. For, if . . . if this was a cemetery, what was the living doing here?

Look! Take it easy! Take it easy! he thought. Better take a drink and forget this girl. You didn't make her your business before, she ain't your business now.

But it was not really the girl on his mind now, but he, himself. He went and poured himself a drink of scotch. He took two drinks, and still the question came: What was he doing here?

Philo went inside and turned on his stereo, turning the volume up loudly. The neighbours wouldn't say anything. They knew he was a calypsonian, and they expected from him not only difference – flair, colour – but vulgarity. This morning he was prepared to make use of the licence they offered even though he knew that the granting of it derived not so much from recognition of his genius (and hence his need for more space, less restraints) as much as the awarding of liberty to one they suffered being among them, one who did not have the training to live with the same gentility the life they lived in Diego Martin.

Today he would use it. And he turned up the volume even a pitch higher than ordinarily because right then he didn't care too greatly if he offended them, in a way, even wanting to outrage them, to scandalize them. He put on some of his old records, singles from way back to The Axe Man, took a bottle of wine from his cabinet, telephoned Jo Ann, and sat on the floor, leafing through his photograph album, sipping wine, listening to the records and waiting for Jo Ann to come over, not even realizing that he had begun a ceremony geared not to stop his nostalgia but to encourage it; and he found himself forced back to his earlier life, back, until he caught glimpses of his childhood on Calvary Hill, a life that came cloudily and jerkily as an illegitimate secret, suppressed for so long, guarded against even his very own self.

And he was seeing his mother, Mother Philomen, a huge Trojan woman, dominating the household of the eight of them by her sullenness and strength and the blue head tie and the blue apron and the chord around her waist that signified that she was a Mother in the Baptist Church and the knowledge that it was the sale of her sugarcakes and mauby and tarts that fed the children and put clothes on their backs and even bought the rum that his father – Neil – had taken to drinking.

He was seeing her now, her round, solemn face beneath the blue headtie, a blue that for all the years never lost its colour, remained clear, distinctive like her sullenness, unfolding, with no hurry at all, her folding chair and setting up, just in front Calvary Hill R.C. School, her table upon which he or his bigger brother deposited the glass case with the sugarcakes and tarts before they went to school, receiving from her no acknowledgement of thanks, rather a solemn stare that suggested that they were undergoing a penance with which it was necessary that they be afflicted if they were not to turn out like their father who, by the time Philo was old enough to carry the glass case on his head, had become a thin, humble, enduring and defeated drunk whose unapplauded and mirthless jokes were at the same time the affirming of his presence and the acknowledgement of his defeat.

He had been, it seems, a cabinet maker, for there were tools of this trade scattered about the house and below it, tools which he could never find when he needed them. Searching for his tools was about the only activity that brought him into contact with his children, and he made it the occasion for his meek and joking try at being boss of the house:

'Where is my sandpaper? Phillip! Rodney! Marcia! Where my sandpaper is? So nobody don't know where my sandpaper is, eh?' Then the sternness would leave his voice as if the performance was too much for him: 'Nobody know the trouble I see. Nobody know . . . Sandpaper! Sandpaper, speak to me, I'm not a beast.'

His mother refused on such occasions to stir herself. She communicated with him in various tones of silences, and the singing of snatches of hymns to express her mood and to comment on his actions, filling the house with her spiritual Baptist rhythm voiced in an undertone that made her sound like the soft plucking of a box bass in a parang band; and yet, she could sing; she could shout; she could talk and bring God himself to the altar of her church when she walked there, filled with rhythmic tremblings and sighs, her cries reaching out like guitar fingers to pluck chords of woe and jubilation from the congregation; but for his father, only her various silences and her humming bass undertones. As if she was weary finally, had been herself defeated by some strength, some stubbornness, in her husband, and could not rely upon her ordinary voice to communicate anything to him. She had to cry in falsetto whispers; that was her sound. Defeated maybe by the cabinet maker who refused to find his tools, who when he found them and occupied himself at his trade, would build cuatros.

He built painstakingly and well the occasional cuatro for which he would be paid in drinks of rum at a rum shop somewhere in Port of Spain, and then he would come home drunk and, turning to his own instrument – the one he left at home, his own cuatro – he would begin to tune it for hours until a string popped or some part of it broke and with the breaking of it, he would go searching, asking for his tools again. And, in answer to his wife's insistent query, which he understood though it was delivered in silence – for they had been together for years, and he had mastered the language which possibly, he had driven her to invent; in answer to her query about the money from the sale of the cuatro, in the midst of searching for his tools, he would suddenly say: 'Eh-eh! You know the scamp ain't pay me for that cuatro yet,' the very sound of his voice pleading to be believed, received by another of his wife's silences, not even a grunt, the sound of which showed that she did not even bother to speculate whether there was any truth at all in what he was saying. Philo used to wonder why his father bothered to say anything at all.

His father lived his life, trying to offset a sense of defeat, by being a comic, trying in an already apologizing voice to make those around him laugh:

'Spell Chicago,' he would ask one of his children, and when they faltered, he would supply the answer: 'A chicken in a car and a car can't go.'

'Spell go,' he would challenge.

'G-O.'

'Spell at.'

'A-T.'

'Join them!'

'Go-At.'

'No. Goat.'

It was as if this kind of humour was all the communication he dared attempt with his children in the presence of his wife. It was as if all the other lessons he had learned from being alive were already ruled out as being of no value to them, where they would be going. He was as a man washed up among travellers going to a land he had never imagined, far less visited. He was lost among them, could make no contribution, provide no guidance. All he could attempt was to amuse them during the interlude they shared.

There was a show that was broadcast on the radio, Local Talent on Parade. Philo's father had entered that show ceaselessly, playing on every occasion a different instrument, or singing, or reciting. Now he would play the cuatro, next the guitar; he would play a saw with a violin fiddle, he would play a tune with his hands cupped over the end of a broken bottle; he would whistle, recite and sing. There were three songs he used to sing: The Rose of Tralee, Ole Man River, and How Deep is the Ocean. He used to recite: Tell me not in mournful numbers that life is but an empty dream . . .

Maybe Philo's mother had heard his performances years before, though now he never sang inside the house, nor recited, only tuned his cuatro until a string burst; but she never betrayed any desire to stay up to hear him over the radio, which the neighbours next door at the appropriate hour turned up loud enough for them to hear Sam Ghany say:

'It's Local Talent on Parade! . . . And now on to contestant number six. We have with us once again Neil Sampson. And what are you going to do for us this time. Neil?'

And his father would reply, switching into a kind of bastard American accent which all the contestants used, perhaps in imitation of Sam Ghany: 'Ah'm gonna play da harmonica – The Breeze and I.'

In all his years of appearing on these shows, his father never won first place. He never placed second either. Fourth. That was his spot. He almost always won a consolation prize: ten cakes of toilet soap, a bottle of after-shave lotion, a pen and pencil set. It seemed as if, like his jokes, his appearances on these shows and others – he appeared sometimes on Auntie Kay's Father's Day show – was a statement that he was present, a kind of insistent cry that he existed. Long afterwards, when Philo was a young calypsonian, caught in the seeming mediocrity of his offering, going from year to year without ever winning a place in the preliminaries of the Calypso King Competition, he had recalled to mind his father in these contests, and had

wondered whether he had not inherited from him a sense
of failure, an ability to be satisfied in the absence of
triumph.

His father died and was buried and was forgotten,
mourned most by his mother who kept on reproaching him
still, not so much with silence as with those short snatches
of falsetto voiced hymns, reminding the six of them, his
sisters and brothers, of their condition, in a speech each
one of them soon knew by heart:

'Your father didn't leave nutten excep' a cuatro without
string and a rusty mout' organ . . . I can't even fine his
tools. So all all-you could depend on to take you through
this world is God, and good manners, since it look to me
like none o' all-you intend to take een education.'

Philo was seeing himself now, and it was early morning
and they were holding his hands, leading him, 'cause he
had a blindfold over his eyes, and they were singing,
making drum rhythm sounds with their voices, and he was
walking, not enough in tune with the spirit, he felt,
because he didn't know whether he really wanted them to
baptize him in this cold river this early morning, because
he had already made his first communion as a Roman
Catholic, but his mother had said that the reason why she
make him turn Catholic was not because Catholic was his
religion, but because he would need every help he could
get in the world, so she had bought the white clothes for
him and he had sung Come Holy Ghost, with other
children, and that was okay. Nobody could arrest him, but
he was frightened here now because any time the police
could come and they would have to run, and he didn't like
the idea of being there at the edge of the river this early
morning with this whispering singing and don't know,
can't see nothing, not even if the police coming. And,
another thing, he didn't like the fellars in school teasing
him that he was Baptist.

Maybe it was his face. He had that kinda face that
challenged, that questioned, that reflected anger, hurt,

resentment. And he was thin too – too thin, too small; his muscles were too small for him to have that kinda face. A fellar would look at him and want to clout him just because he had that kinda face, that kinda look about him. But, he would fight back. He was not a good fighter, but he would fight back. And he had to do a lot of fighting back because he was too sensitive to what they called jokes. To tease him that his mother sold sugarcakes and tarts was a joke, and that he carried the glass case on his head was a joke; it was a joke that he was Baptist, and that he was black and skinny was a joke. He didn't like jokes. They used every weapon at their disposal to make him learn, as they put it, to take jokes. They gave him a nickname in every class he passed through, as if his schoolfellows needed to identify him anew, name him again for himself and them. And though he was skinny, he would argue and fight, resist becoming what they wanted him to be.

Every Friday evening he would have his hands full at the back of the school where his mother couldn't see him. His anger, his rage, was great, but he had little skill, and he hardly ever won a fight; and sometimes the boys carried on the fight with him simply because he wouldn't give in. In a way the boys didn't even want to fight him. They wanted not to defeat him so much as to defeat the sensitivity in him, to make him, as it were, take jokes. He refused. And when he couldn't hold out any longer, when he was tired fighting and getting beaten and being made the butt of the jokes among boys who were no less black nor less Baptist nor less poor than he, he surrendered. He began to turn the jokes upon himself. It was he who gave himself the name, Philo. They used to call him Miss Philomen son 'Call me Philo,' he said. He became a clown whose brutality to himself brought laughter. He ridiculed his mother's sugarcakes and tarts: 'Aye, boy!' he would shout in alarm, 'you eating *those* sugarcakes? You know how we does make them sugarcakes? Every morning we does get up early to chew the coconut. Then all o' we does spit out the chewed-up coconut in the pot, then my mother make the sugarcakes.' He made fun of carrying the glass case on his head – that was why he was so dunce, he said. That he was black was a great joke. Everything that he had tried to rebel against he now made a joke of.

A fellar would say: 'The ugliest fellar go for water.'

And Philo would respond: 'I ain't going.'

He became a clown in school. And that brought him the attention of the schoolmaster, Mr Grimes.

'SAMUEL! Come here!'

There were two trees in the schoolyard, a downes tree and a tamarind tree. The downes tree provided fruit for the children, the tamarind tree provided, apart from fruit, whips.

'Go and cut two whips for me.'

Philo would cut the whips, choosing the best, swishing them through the air, testing them himself for suppleness, for length and strength; for, if either broke at the schoolmaster's testing, not only would he have to go and cut another one, but the number of strokes he would receive would be increased. He would return and give the whips to Mr Grimes and begin the drama that he managed to make of these floggings, before the entire school.

'Thank you.' Mr Grimes always said thank you after he had tested the whips and found them to his liking.

Then would come the dance.

'Come!' Mr Grimes would say. 'Come here, Samuel!'

And backing away, Philo would begin his loud mocking pleading: 'Sir! Yes, sir! I coming sir. Spare me, sir! Sir, I wouldn't do it again Mr Grimes, sir. Sir, God will bless you if you don't beat me, sir . . .'

'Come!' Mr Grimes would say, advancing upon him.

'Sir, I feeling weak, sir. I feeling sick. Sir, I wanto pee! I wanto pee, sir! Sir!'

'Come!'

'Sir, I will pee my pants, sir. Sir! Sir, I peeing my pants already, sir! I don't want to pee my pants right here, sir!

Sir, you mean you going to beat me and I peeing my pants already, sir! Sir?'

'Come, boy!'

'I coming, sir. But I don't want you to beat me, sir!'

When Mr Grimes finally held him and began to whip him, he would jump and holler at the top of his voice: 'Oh God-O! Oh God-O! Murder! Murder! Whey! Oww! Lord! Ah going to dead! Sir, you killing me, Sir! Murder! Murder!'

And Mr Grimes saying, 'Hush! Hush! Shut up! Shut up!' and flogging him harder.

As soon as the flogging ended, all his cries ceased. He went back to his seat jauntily, whispering loud enough for the whole class to hear: 'You know this man wanto kill me! He going to kill me one day, you know!'

His schoolfellows admired him.

'Philo, you don't feel those whips, boy?'

'Feel? What name feel?'

'You mean you really ain't 'fraid licks?'

''Fraid licks?'

He became a kind of star, fellars looked up to him, and now he could even scare fellars bigger than he was. 'I ain't 'fraid licks, you know.' That became his anthem and warning and bluff.

Later when he began to sing calypsos he would retain that theme, that theme of toughness, the ability to withstand punishment, a bluffing mockery at himself and those who punished him.

> *Since I know myself people beating me*
> *I asking them why they wouldn't tell me*
> *At last I know why, is because I don't cry*
> *Bobolee don't have water in their eye.*

> *So beat me again*
> *I wouldn't complain*
> *Break off my hands, bust up my shins*

'Cause I won't cry, and you know why
Bobolee don't have water in their eye.

He didn't sing for the tourist so much then, if they came in the tent to listen, let them walk with a Trinidad dictionary. But the MC felt it was a good song and used to explain to strangers that bobolee was a sort of effigy of Judas, fellars got an old jacket and old pants and stuffed it up with straw to beat on Good Friday, and all the boys with big sticks beating it and running behind it, crying: 'Beat! Beat! Beat the bobolee!'

The devil ain't bad like me 'cause I blacker than he
They want to belittle me by comparing him to me
He never went to jail and he only breathe fire out his mout'
But I have fire coming out my tail.

This was the quality of his offering until at forty-two he came up with The Axe Man. And maybe if it wasn't for the rain that night he might never have sung it. But that night the crowd wasn't big and the MC wasn't good at all, though maybe even Lord Melody himself, if he had been there, would have had trouble keeping them from steupsing. They were booing everything. And they was right because that night it looked like every calypsonian had decided to sing something slow and cold like the weather; so he thought that he might as well sing it and get booed too. The thing about the song that worried him was that it didn't fit him. He was skinny and ordinary and unmuscular. He didn't look nothing like the Axe Man. So he sang it with a lot of spirit, like he was making a kinda joke; but it had a good bouncy tune and before he was finished, people was applauding. They went crazy. He thought it was a fluke. But next night the crowd was applauding again, and the next night, all through the season, right to the finals of the King Competition. He had hit on something.

A professor of English at the University of the West

Indies explained it for him in an article some time afterwards:

'Of all the areas of human endeavour, the rulers of the world had granted to the Black man the penis of which he would be sole and undeniable ruler. In projecting himself as The Great Fucker, Philo has managed to hit on an area of affirming what was already granted him. We ought not to wonder at his appeal.'

I am the axe man cutting forests down
I am the axe man working all over town
If you have a tree to cut I am the man to call
I never put my axe on a tree and it didn't break and fall.

The next year he came out with Women Running Me Down:

All over town, I can't get a rest
Ah never thought I would meet the day when woman is a pest
But I stand up to the test
Because I is the axe man, I is the best.

That, and I Am the Ape Man Not Tarzan won him the Calypso King crown:

I am the ape man not Tarzan
This is something you have to understand
Tarzan couldn't be no ape
Anywhere in Africa he land we woulda cook him for dinner
He couldn't escape.

They just want to make me shame, giving Tarzan my fame
Imagine, this white man swinging from tree to tree
I must laugh at that, how could it be?
Is me! I am the monkey man, not he.

The same professor writing about three years later, after he had won the Calypso King crown for two of those years, harking back to that first really successful season, suggested that it was his Tarzan calypso that really made the turning point for him, really lifted him above the crop of calypsonians of his time. Wrote the professor:

The political and social themes confronted so subtly in Lord Philo's Tarzan calypso had already begun to indicate a cryptic humour and incisive wit that could force open, indeed, explode myths cultivated by the propagandists of the western world to deprive the Black man of his sense of location.

He has shown how ridiculous is the claim of the western world, how overreaching and arrogant it has been to suggest that an European lord would not only survive in the jungle, but prevail as lord of all the African jungle, in harmony with nature, a harmony that the European in practice has long since subverted in favour of scientific dissection, a practice that has increasingly alienated him from himself.

Philo has in one blow put into perspective the utter ridiculousness of the twin claims: the barbarity of the blacks and the harmony with nature of the whites.

It was a nice article, and he had cut it out and put it into his scrapbook. The calypso that started him along his road to fame and fortune was the Axe Man; for, at forty-two it not only helped to give him his first successful season, it gave him a vision of how he might succeed. He had found a way in which he could affirm himself and survive. It emphasized for him the necessity to be *role* serious, not real serious, and brought him back to his own affirming irreverence that had seen him through his boyhood. He could see jokes in things again. Life wasn't so dully, so wickedly serious again. He wasn't sure that he understood the professor. The point he, Philo, was striving to make in the Tarzan calypso was that the Africans would have eaten Tarzan if he was real. He liked the idea of Africans as cannibals. What a nice wicked sight! Tarzan in a big steaming iron pot and Africans jumping around waiting for him to cook. Any time he listened to that calypso he laughed.

No, Tarzan didn't even rank second. After Axe Man the calypso that consolidated his position as a top singer was the one on the fellars by the Corner: Hooligans In Port of Spain.

That was one time he was real angry. He had gone to Fisheye and Aldrick as friend. He wanted them to understand, to share his good fortune with him. He didn't make life. All he was doing was trying to get through, to make a space for himself in the world. Because he bought some new clothes and a car they viewed him as a traitor. Traitor to what? To what cause? What did they want him to do? Continue to stand on the Corner watching people pass? What did they want him to do? End up like his father singing and playing the arse on Local Talent on Parade? The show didn't even exist any more. Instead of giving him support they were ready to drag him down. They insulted him. They slapped his woman.

This episode always pained him, and he felt the pain now, again. Maybe it would have come anyway. He had to move on, and they couldn't, wouldn't leave the Corner. But, couldn't they have parted ways more sensibly? Couldn't they have parted without the bust up, without the bacchanal? He had to get away, to move in a larger area of space, to move, to move on.

Move on to what? To Diego Martin? He had moved on. Yes!

'Yes!' he whispered aloud as he listened to the calypsos of his moving on. 'Yes!'

> Dirty Janet, black like Jet, wouldn't take a bath
> She face like a tart
> Want me to marry she, boy,
> If you hear how I laugh.

and:

> Poor Emelda, she can't get a lock for she door
> It always open to rich and poor
> I going home the other night, one big uproar
> A sailor, a soldier, a police and a scavenger
> Fighting to get in Emelda door.

and:

> *I hear the Baptists singing, praying for heaven*
> *Waiting for salvation from the Lord*
> *They not working, they only skylarking, making*
> *More hungry children*
> *Waiting for salvation from the Lord.*

and:

> *Bad Johns on the Corner and in night clubs*
> *I ain't 'fraid you again*
> *Yesterday you was bad, today I am the ruler*
> *Of Trinidad.*

'Yes!'

Philo sat and listened to the records spin, his voice sounding in the valley; spin, killing, wounding, vilifying his childhood heroes, his friends, the bad Johns, the Baptists, black women, his mother, his sisters, his self.

Yes, he had moved on:

> *Calvary Hill people their head not right*
> *Cussing every day and looking for fight*
> *How human beings could live there I really don't know*
> *That is why I say, Philo, you have to leave and go.*

Yes, he had moved on. Moved on. He heard a car blowing and he got up and went to the door to see if it was Jo Ann, but also needing the air, needing to move his limbs, stretch.

A man from the neighbourhood was turning his car in Philo's driveway. The fellow took one hand off the steering wheel to wave.

'Hey! Man, don't turn that fucking car on *that* lawn!'

The fellow looked around, confused, shocked, began to struggle with the steering wheel and his gears, and his car stalled.

'This ain't no highway!' Philo shouted, hoping that he would retaliate, say something, anything, so he could get the excuse to give him a good cussing. He didn't like that man. He didn't like none of them. The fellow calmed himself and drove off, half smiling, wondering if Philo was serious or if it was some joke he was making.

'They is the ones! Is them. They is the ones applauding in the tents. They is the ones. . . . Can't even cuss.'

He was still standing there, watching after the fellow had driven away, when Jo Ann drove in.

'You know those bitches don't even know how to cuss. Lookin' at me as if he never hear anybody say, fuck!'

'What happen?' She held his hand, intertwining her fingers with his. She was twenty-three, pretty, polished, casual, elegant, Afro.

'Say fuck!' he said.

She hesitated: 'Fuck,' she said, wondering.

'Com' on, let's fuck!' he said.

'Hey' She smiled, chuckled, looked up at him. 'What happen?' she asked softly.

'I is a' ole nigger, you know. I is a Calvary Hill man. I ain't no hifalutin Diego Martin jackass!'

They walked inside. 'Hey! You playing old records!' She seemed delighted. She sat on the couch and started to undo her blouse. 'What happen?'

'Where these people come from, eh? Tell me, where they was living before they come to live in Diego Martin? Where they come from?'

'Come,' she said, pulling him down on the couch beside her. 'Tell me what happen.'

'Nothing,' he said. 'Nothing.'

She began to unbutton his trousers. 'What is it?'

He got up and turned off the stereo. 'Put on something else, if you want. I don't want to hear those calypsos.'

'But I like them,' she said.

'You ever listen to them?'

'But of course.'

She saw his face, and she said, 'Okay, I don't want no music.'

Afterwards, they lay in bed naked – the couch had suddenly become too small for him, and he had felt the need for space. And he felt tired and not young. And she was gentle in her movements. And they lay without any covers over them, naked in each other's eyes. And he looked at her body, she watching him, and he touched her so gently that he trembled over her smooth thighs. It was the first time they were together like this in the daylight in the eight months they had known each other. And he was a little afraid, for she was young, too young, and he wondered if, seeing him as he was now in the light, without his car and the feather in his hat and his rings on his fingers, if . . . how she would feel.

'You think I disrespect you?' he asked.

She laughed. 'Don't worry, I heard that word before.'

'Not from me. I never say fuck to you.'

'And you not ashamed,' she said, smiling.

'You, your generation, you liberated. I . . . I am old school.'

'You? You not old school.'

And those words pleased him, encouraged him, and he felt kinda glad that he had said 'fuck' to her and that he was naked in full view of her and was naked to himself. He was kinda glad for that.

'You know I am one of them,' he said.

'Who? One of who?'

'These people here, these Diego Martin people.'

'Oh, them.'

'You knew it all the time?'

'Yeah!'

'And you never tell me.'

'Never tell you what?'

'That I was one of them.'

'Well, what's so big about that?' She was puzzled, and he couldn't explain, so he let it rest. And before he knew it, he was talking, telling her of his life, of his childhood, telling about his brother, Mello, who was a promising sportsman, good in every game, but slack, worthless, was stabbed to death by a woman, for what he never got to know. And about his sister who got saved and became Pentecostal and was a preacher, about another sister who went away to America and married a white fellar, and another one who married a policeman and lived in Tunapuna.

'We was Baptist, you know. My mother was always humming, and my father played the cuatro. Guess that's where the music come from.'

'You know, this is the first time you ever tell me anything about yourself,' she said. 'I never knew you had brothers and sisters. I thought you were alone in the world.'

'It was six of us.'

'I thought you had no memories at all.'

He was quiet, thinking. 'You right. I didn't have no memories at all.'

'Like my father,' she said. 'He doesn't have any memories either. All I know about him is that he was in the war.'

Philo grunted. 'You thought I had no memories at all?'

'So help me. Just like Daddy. I tired ask Daddy, "Daddy, tell me something about when you were a boy. Tell me about your parents." And somehow, he never had nothing to tell. As if he really didn't remember. But how can a person not have memories?'

'We kill them.' He was thinking of his calypsos. 'We murder them.'

'But how can you kill them? You kill yourself if you kill them. How do you live when you kill them?'

'Copy, invent, imitate. Me, I'm an imitator and an imaginator and a fabricator. That is how I live here. Listen, when I was a boy . . .' And he told her about his boyhood, about the jokes and the fighting and the whippings from Mr Grimes, and about his surrender.

She pulled the covers over them, and she held him

gently, motherly, as if to hush him, hide him from himself.

'No. I don't want the covers. You cover yourself if you want to.'

'I don't want them either. It was for you.'

'For me?' And again he was touched by this young woman. 'For me? No. Let me be naked before you. Let me be naked.'

So he lay there naked and silent.

'But, what could you do? You had to stay alive,' she said. 'Those boys woulda killed you.'

He thought of his calypsos and of his mother and father and of his own self. He felt tears coming up into his nostrils. Then he chuckled. 'They didn't kill me.'

'No. You alive.'

'I'm alive? Alive? Alive, you said?'

'You couldn't do anything else.'

'Yeah, I couldn't do anything else. Yeah,' lazily, tiredly.

'Stop it, Philo! Stop it! Stop it, please. You couldn't do anything else. . . . What could you do?'

They fool me again, he thought, thinking of Diego Martin. They fool me again, the idea sounding like the beginning of another calypso.

'You know what I want to do,' he said, after a while. 'I want to love. I want to live,' not moving to touch the girl. 'I want to love.'

'I . . . I want . . .' She didn't complete what she was saying. She rolled over and hugged him around his chest.

'You're a nice girl,' he said.

'You're a nice man,' she said.

They fell asleep, and when he awoke she was still sleeping, and it was night. He got up and dressed quickly, quietly so as not to awaken her. He kissed her on the forehead when he was leaving, feeling sad, feeling romantic, feeling soft. It was raining outside, and he got into his car and headed for the city.

He drove up Calvary Hill slowly, watching through the

falling rain, the lights, the houses, seeing blurs. He wasn't wearing his hat with the feather in it. He parked near Freddie's snackette and got out in the rain.

He stood before the place, suddenly frightened. Then he went in out of the rain, feeling that he was entering a home to which he had forfeited any welcome. He had come here on an impulse, and he stood at the counter, suddenly awkward, waiting, as if in so doing his purpose would be revealed to him. He called for a petit quart of rum and stood at the counter with it.

'Hey! Is you? Is you? Philo! Philo!'

To his surprise he was overwhelmed by greetings. Everybody came over and slapped him on the back and shook his limp hands. And he was watching them, wondering if they were putting him on, thinking: 'How come they do not see that I'm a traitor.' He was on his guard still. He wanted to apologize to them, but he didn't have the guts to do it. The words wouldn't come into his mouth. They played his calypsos on the juke box and they offered him drinks. And he drank them as if they were poison he would have to take.

And then he thought: 'What would my apology be worth?' And he knew that it was not a selfish thought, that it was not for himself alone he was thinking that, but for them too. And he thought, maybe there is nothing to apologize for; the thing is to live and to grow on, not even to think that you could right wrongs, but grow on, take it from here.

> *Take it from here*
> *Just where I am a traitor and betrayer*
> *without memories or self*
> *I want to remember and hold you*
> *and love you . : .*

The calypso came quick. Or maybe it was not a calypso, but a poem to be understood by being felt.

'I love you,' he said, in his showman kinda way, turning

to leave, and wishing that he could have said it better, said it softer and in his own voice, like to a woman, and not with the kinda American accent he used for his shows. 'I love you!'

Outside, the rain still falling, he felt that he would come back another time and try to say it better.

When he left there, Philo drove up to Alice Street. Cleothilda's house was locked, but there was a light on. He knocked on the door.

'Is me, Philo!' he answered to her inquiry.

She opened for him.

'What you doing here this hour?' A drowsy delight was in her voice, and she held out her two hands and drew him inside. 'Come in! Sit down!'

'I was just passing through, so I drop in to see you. How you?'

She sighed.

He sat there not knowing what to say. Indeed, he had nothing to say.

'You sure nothing ain't happen? What happen?'

'I tell you, I was just passing through. So I can't drop in to look for you?'

'You want a drink?'

He nodded.

'It chilly tonight, eh?' she said, bringing the drink, and sitting opposite him, pulling a shawl about her shoulders.

He nodded.

She studied him closely. And she put an index finger in her mouth and let her eyelids flutter coquettishly. 'I know what happen,' she said triumphantly, 'you going away, and you come to bring a little present for me before you leave.'

'Yes,' he said. 'I going away.'

'You know,' she said, more comfortable that she understood him, 'you know, you lucky to meet me up at this hour. All now I would be dreaming, but, tonight I can't sleep. I sit down here thinking how the world funny so . . . You know Guy come back from England since yesterday. You know he went to a conference (see how big the boy get). He come back yesterday, bring all the things for the wedding. He ain't see Sylvia yet . . . You know her mother sick in hospital. Well he, Guy, think she gone to carry her mother over by her sister in Belmont. He bring all sorta fancy things for her, and whole day he looking out for her. Only trouble is Sylvia ain't gone by no mother. You know,' she said, her voice descending to a whisper, 'that girl gone to look for Aldrick. But with all the presents and things Guy bring, I ain't have the guts to tell him anything.'

Philo sat back. He had finished his drink.

'You want another one?'

He nodded.

'And we better go inside I feeling a bit chilly out here.'

He got up slowly.

'Come,' she said, stretching out a hand for him to hold. 'You doing like if you don't know where my bedroom is. But with the way the world going, even that wouldn't surprise me,' she said in a voice as if the world was truly coming to an end.